Venus and Mars ru... and passion. The po... planets at birth reveals a lover's deepest desires and secrets, determines his basic love group, and tells if it blends with yours. Nothing is hidden. All you need is a correct birthdate, and this book.

NOTHING IS HIDDEN

Star Signs tell you the *Venus and Mars Aspect* of your lover—the combination that rules romance, love and passion *only*! Star Signs are very specific and deep; they are not about appearances or surface qualities shared by millions of others (Oh, he's a Libra..."). Star Signs are accurate because they are based on the year of birth. They let you look deeper, behind the eyes, into the very heart...

You must have the correct year of birth. Check a driver's license if possible. People usually tell the truth about their birth month, but will sometimes lie about the year.

Please do not show the reading to the subject. Star Signs are secrets. They are the truth, and the truth can be painful. Star Signs should be used to keep you from getting hurt, not to hurt others.

STAR SIGNS TELL YOU
WHAT YOU NEED TO KNOW
IN ONE MINUTE!

**SUPPOSE YOU MEET SOMEONE
WHOSE BIRTHDAY IS APRIL 11, 1952**

(1) FIRST TURN TO THE CHARTS for 1952 and find April 11 in both columns...

1952

Venus   *Mars*

Apr 9—May 3 Aries   Jan 20—Aug 26   Scorpio

Venus in Aries and *Mars in Scorpio* are the Star Signs for this lover.

(2) THEN TURN TO THE *TABLE OF COMBINATIONS,* and find...

Venus in Aries and Mars in Scorpio 100

(3) NOW TURN TO THE *READING* on page 100, where you quickly find out that this lover is *erratic* in Romance ("This one makes war, is relentless..."), *chaotic* in Love ("...love is a lure!"), *tumultuous* in Passion ("Sends shivers..."). You are advised to *play this one short term* as *you can get hurt*! You also learn that this lover is in group C and blends with groups A and B but *not* with D or other C's.

STAR SIGNS

⟨FOR⟩

LOVERS

The Venus
and Mars Aspect

ROBERT WORTH

A Life-Saving Guide
to Romance, Love & Passion

A BERKLEY BOOK
published by
BERKLEY PUBLISHING CORPORATION

This Berkley book contains the complete
text of the original hardcover edition.
It has been completely reset in a type face
designed for easy reading, and was printed
from new film.

STAR SIGNS FOR LOVERS

A Berkley Book / published by arrangement with
Chelsea House Publishers

PRINTING HISTORY
Chelsea House edition published December 1978
Berkley edition / July 1979

ISBN: 0-425-04238-3

A BERKLEY BOOK ® TM 757,375
Berkley Books are published by Berkley Publishing Corporation,
200 Madison Avenue, New York, New York 10016.
PRINTED IN THE UNITED STATES OF AMERICA

Contents

Star Signs for Lovers
(The Guide)

The Guide is a unique fast-working life saving astrology book.

The Guide enables you to see into people.

The Guide describes romance, love and passion as it is in everyone.

Tells what to expect.

Tells what to do.

The Guide is a book of prescriptions.

The Guide is a compass.

Use it.

Trust it.

Nobody is going to fool you any more.

Nobody is going to hurt you any more.

Nobody is going to waste your time.

The Venus & Mars Aspect

Venus and Mars are the two planets that relate to romance, love and passion. These planets travel through the signs constantly. The Guide tells in what signs Venus and Mars were placed at any date. (Everyone in the world had Venus and Mars placed in the twelve signs at birth.) Where Venus and Mars were placed and what it means is what The Guide is all about.

There are 144 possible combinations. Everyone in the world is one of the 144 combinations. The 144 combinations are a mini-horoscope of every human being: a picture of romance, love and passion as it is in everyone.

The Guide describes each combination, tells what to expect, what to do.

Some Background

The planets of the solar system move constantly. As the planets move they form patterns. When you were born the planets were in a pattern. No pattern is repeated. That is why there is only one you, why each human being is different.

There are the Sun and the Moon, eight planets, twelve signs of the Zodiac. The Guide deals with just two of the planets in the signs. There is nothing difficult, no mathematics. It's easy. Simple. Instant. You don't have to be an expert.

How to Find
the Combination of Your Lover

Get the birth date, exact day, month and year. A partial birth date (just day and month) is not sufficient. "I'm a Capricorn" is not enough information. The Guide doesn't deal with sun signs. It doesn't deal with outer images. Sun signs offer only superficial information, the outer style and physical appearance. You cannot put everyone in the world into twelve general categories and expect to know the inner flow of each person.

You can look into the eyes of a Capricorn, a Gemini or a Virgo and never know what's going on. The Guide takes you behind the eyes.

The exact birth date is essential. Be smart in getting it. Be subtle. People lie about their age. Get your hands on a driver's license if you can. Or a passport.

You can't afford to make a judgment based on inaccurate information. The Guide is keyed to the exact birth date. The day, the month, and the year.

How to Work the Guide

Turn to The Charts, pages 1–73. Find the right year. Look up the month and the day. Get the placement of Venus. Then get the placement of Mars. Write them both down.

Go to the Table of Combinations, pages 75–83. Find the page number for the combination you want a reading on. That person's inner flow will be revealed to you.

Now you are on your own.

Don't discuss The Guide with your subject. Don't discuss the combinations. Love is dangerous. The Guide is full of secrets. The game is to win, to find your happiness. How you do it is your own business.

Keep The Guide with you. Refer to it for each new encounter. The Guide will never let you down.

Good luck.

How to Work the Charts
(An Example)

The Charts tell where Venus and Mars were placed from 1895 through 1965.

Suppose the birth date you want a reading on is November 9, 1957. Go to the year first, then find the month and day in both tables.

turn the page

1957

Venus

Jan 1—Jan 12	Sagittarius
Jan 13—Feb 5	Capricorn
Feb 6—Mar 1	Aquarius
Mar 2—Mar 25	Pisces
Mar 26—Apr 19	Aries
Apr 20—May 13	Taurus
May 14—Jun 6	Gemini
Jun 7—Jul 1	Cancer
Jul 2—Jul 26	Leo
Jul 27—Aug 19	Virgo
Aug 20—Sep 14	Libra
Sep 15—Oct 9	Scorpio
Oct 10—Nov 4	Sagittarius
Nov 5—Dec 6	Capricorn
Dec 7—Dec 31	Aquarius

Mars

Jan 1—Jan 28	Aries
Jan 29—Mar 17	Taurus
Mar 18—May 4	Gemini
May 5—Jun 21	Cancer
Jun 22—Aug 8	Leo
Aug 9—Sep 24	Libra
Nov 9—Dec 23	Scorpio
Dec 24—Dec 31	Sagittarius

From November 5 through December 6 Venus was in Capricorn.

From November 9 through December 23 Mars was in Scorpio.

The combination is VENUS IN CAPRICORN and MARS IN SCORPIO.

Go to the Table of Combinations for that aspect, (page 81).

See page 316.

STAR SIGNS FOR LOVERS

The Venus
and Mars Aspect

E. Karlin

The Charts

1895

Venus

Jan 1—Jan 10	Capricorn
Jan 11—Feb 3	Aquarius
Feb 4—Feb 27	Pisces
Feb 28—Mar 23	Aries
Mar 24—Apr 17	Taurus
Apr 18—May 12	Gemini
May 13—Jun 7	Cancer
Jun 8—Jul 6	Leo
Jul 7—Aug 13	Virgo
Aug 14—Sep 12	Libra
Sep 13—Nov 6	Virgo
Nov 7—Dec 8	Libra
Dec 9—Dec 31	Scorpio

Mars

Jan 1—Mar 1	Taurus
Mar 2—Apr 21	Gemini
Apr 22—Jun 10	Cancer
Jun 11—Jul 28	Leo
Jul 29—Sep 13	Virgo
Sep 14—Oct 29	Libra
Oct 30—Dec 11	Scorpio
Dec 12—Dec 31	Sagittarius

Turn to the Table of Combinations.
Find page for the combination.

1896

Venus

Jan 1—Jan 3	Scorpio
Jan 4—Jan 29	Sagittarius
Jan 30—Feb 23	Capricorn
Feb 24—Mar 18	Aquarius
Mar 19—Apr 12	Pisces
Apr 13—May 6	Aries
May 7—May 31	Taurus
Jun 1—Jun 24	Gemini
Jun 25—Jul 19	Cancer
Jul 20—Aug 12	Leo
Aug 13—Sep 5	Virgo
Sep 6—Sep 29	Libra
Sep 30—Oct 24	Scorpio
Oct 25—Nov 17	Sagittarius
Nov 18—Dec 12	Capricorn
Dec 13—Dec 31	Aquarius

Mars

Jan 1—Jan 22	Sagittarius
Jan 23—Mar 2	Capricorn
Mar 3—Apr 11	Aquarius
Apr 12—May 21	Pisces
May 22—Jul 1	Aries
Jul 2—Aug 15	Taurus
Aug 16—Dec 31	Gemini

Turn to the Table of Combinations.
Find page for the combination.

4

1897

Venus

Jan 1—Jan 6	Aquarius
Jan 7—Feb 1	Pisces
Feb 2—Mar 4	Aries
Mar 5—Jul 7	Taurus
Jul 8—Aug 5	Gemini
Aug 6—Aug 31	Cancer
Sep 1—Sep 26	Leo
Sep 27—Oct 20	Virgo
Oct 21—Nov 13	Libra
Nov 14—Dec 7	Scorpio
Dec 8—Dec 31	Sagittarius

Mars

Jan 1—Mar 21	Gemini
Mar 22—May 17	Cancer
May 18—Jul 8	Leo
Jul 9—Aug 25	Virgo
Aug 26—Oct 9	Libra
Oct 10—Nov 21	Scorpio
Nov 22—Dec 31	Sagittarius

Turn to the Table of Combinations.
Find page for the combination.

1898

Venus

Jan 1—Jan 24	Capricorn
Jan 25—Feb 17	Aquarius
Feb 18—Mar 13	Pisces
Mar 14—Apr 6	Aries
Apr 7—May 1	Taurus
May 2—May 25	Gemini
May 26—Jun 19	Cancer
Jun 20—Jul 14	Leo
Jul 15—Aug 10	Virgo
Aug 11—Sep 16	Libra
Sep 17—Oct 7	Scorpio
Oct 8—Dec 31	Sagittarius

Mars

Jan 1	Sagittarius
Jan 2—Feb 10	Capricorn
Feb 11—Mar 20	Aquarius
Mar 21—Apr 28	Pisces
Apr 29—Jun 6	Aries
Jun 7—Jul 18	Taurus
Jul 19—Sep 2	Gemini
Sep 3—Oct 30	Cancer
Oct 31—Dec 31	Leo

Turn to the Table of Combinations.
Find page for the combination.

1899

Venus		*Mars*	
Jan 1—Feb 5	Sagittarius	Jan 1—Jan 15	Leo
Feb 6—Mar 5	Capricorn	Jan 16—Apr 14	Cancer
Mar 6—Mar 31	Aquarius	Apr 15—Jun 15	Leo
Apr 1—Apr 26	Pisces	Jun 16—Aug 5	Virgo
Apr 27—May 21	Aries	Aug 6—Sep 20	Libra
May 22—Jun 15	Taurus	Sep 21—Nov 2	Scorpio
Jun 16—Jul 10	Gemini	Nov 3—Dec 13	Sagittarius
Jul 11—Aug 3	Cancer	Dec 14—Dec 31	Capricorn
Aug 4—Aug 28	Leo		
Aug 29—Sep 21	Virgo		
Sep 22—Oct 15	Libra		
Oct 16—Nov 8	Scorpio		
Nov 9—Dec 2	Sagittarius		
Dec 3—Dec 26	Capricorn		
Dec 27—Dec 31	Aquarius		

Turn to the Table of Combinations.
Find page for the combination.

1900

Venus

Jan 1—Jan 19	Aquarius
Jan 20—Feb 13	Pisces
Feb 14—Mar 10	Aries
Mar 11—Apr 5	Taurus
Apr 6—May 5	Gemini
May 6—Sep 8	Cancer
Sep 9—Oct 8	Leo
Oct 9—Nov 3	Virgo
Nov 4—Nov 28	Libra
Nov 29—Dec 22	Scorpio
Dec 23—Dec 31	Sagittarius

Mars

Jan 1—Jan 22	Capricorn
Jan 23—Feb 28	Aquarius
Mar 1—Apr 7	Pisces
Apr 8—May 16	Aries
May 17—Jun 26	Taurus
Jun 27—Aug 9	Gemini
Aug 10—Sep 26	Cancer
Sep 27—Nov 22	Leo
Nov 23—Dec 31	Virgo

Turn to the Table of Combinations.
Find page for the combination.

1901

Venus

Jan 1—Jan 15	Sagittarius
Jan 16—Feb 9	Capricorn
Feb 10—Mar 5	Aquarius
Mar 6—Mar 29	Pisces
Mar 30—Apr 22	Aries
Apr 23—May 16	Taurus
May 17—Jun 10	Gemini
Jun 11—Jul 4	Cancer
Jul 5—Jul 29	Leo
Jul 30—Aug 23	Virgo
Aug 24—Sep 16	Libra
Sep 17—Oct 12	Scorpio
Oct 13—Nov 7	Sagittarius
Nov 8—Dec 5	Capricorn
Dec 6—Dec 31	Aquarius

Mars

Jan 1—Mar 1	Virgo
Mar 2—May 10	Leo
May 11—Jul 13	Virgo
Jul 14—Aug 31	Libra
Sep 1—Oct 14	Scorpio
Oct 15—Nov 23	Sagittarius
Nov 24—Dec 31	Capricorn

Turn to the Table of Combinations.
Find page for the combination.

1902

Venus		*Mars*	
Jan 1—Jan 11	Aquarius	Jan 1	Capricorn
Jan 12—Feb 6	Pisces	Jan 2—Feb 8	Aquarius
Feb 7—Apr 4	Aquarius	Feb 9—Mar 18	Pisces
Apr 5—May 6	Pisces	Mar 19—Apr 26	Aries
May 7—Jun 3	Aries	Apr 27—Jun 6	Taurus
Jun 4—Jun 29	Taurus	Jun 7—Jul 20	Gemini
Jun 30—Jul 25	Gemini	Jul 21—Sep 4	Cancer
Jul 26—Aug 19	Cancer	Sep 5—Oct 23	Leo
Aug 20—Sep 12	Leo	Oct 24—Dec 19	Virgo
Sep 13—Oct 7	Virgo	Dec 20—Dec 31	Libra
Oct 8—Oct 30	Libra		
Oct 31—Nov 23	Scorpio		
Nov 24—Dec 17	Sagittarius		
Dec 18—Dec 31	Capricorn		

Turn to the Table of Combinations.
Find page for the combination.

1903

Venus

Jan 1—Jan 10	Capricorn
Jan 11—Feb 3	Aquarius
Feb 4—Feb 27	Pisces
Feb 28—Mar 23	Aries
Mar 24—Apr 17	Taurus
Apr 18—May 13	Gemini
May 14—Jun 8	Cancer
Jun 9—Jul 17	Leo
Jul 8—Aug 17	Virgo
Aug 18—Sep 6	Libra
Sep 7—Nov 8	Virgo
Nov 9—Dec 9	Libra
Dec 10—Dec 31	Scorpio

Mars

Jan 1—Apr 19	Libra
Apr 20—May 30	Virgo
May 31—Aug 6	Libra
Aug 7—Sep 22	Scorpio
Sep 23—Nov 2	Sagittarius
Nov 3—Dec 11	Capricorn
Dec 12—Dec 31	Aquarius

Turn to the Table of Combinations.
Find page for the combination.

1904

Venus		*Mars*	
Jan 1—Jan 4	Scorpio	Jan 1—Jan 19	Aquarius
Jan 5—Jan 29	Sagittarius	Jan 20—Feb 26	Pisces
Jan 30—Feb 23	Capricorn	Feb 27—Apr 6	Aries
Feb 24—Mar 19	Aquarius	Apr 7—May 17	Taurus
Mar 20—Apr 12	Pisces	May 18—Jun 30	Gemini
Apr 13—May 7	Aries	Jul 1—Aug 14	Cancer
May 8—May 31	Taurus	Aug 15—Oct 1	Leo
Jun 1—Jun 25	Gemini	Oct 2—Nov 19	Virgo
Jun 26—Jul 19	Cancer	Nov 20—Dec 31	Libra
Jul 20—Aug 12	Leo		
Aug 13—Sep 6	Virgo		
Sep 7—Sep 30	Libra		
Oct 1—Oct 24	Scorpio		
Oct 25—Nov 18	Sagittarius		
Nov 19—Dec 12	Capricorn		
Dec 13—Dec 31	Aquarius		

Turn to the Table of Combinations.
Find page for the combination.

1905

Venus

Jan 1—Jan 7	Aquarius
Jan 8—Feb 2	Pisces
Feb 3—Mar 5	Aries
Mar 6—May 8	Taurus
May 9—May 27	Aries
May 28—Jul 7	Taurus
Jul 8—Aug 5	Gemini
Aug 6—Sep 1	Cancer
Sep 2—Sep 26	Leo
Sep 27—Oct 21	Virgo
Oct 22—Nov 14	Libra
Nov 15—Dec 8	Scorpio
Dec 9—Dec 31	Sagittarius

Mars

Jan 1—Jan 13	Libra
Jan 14—Aug 21	Scorpio
Aug 22—Oct 7	Sagittarius
Oct 8—Nov 17	Capricorn
Nov 18—Dec 27	Aquarius
Dec 28—Dec 31	Pisces

Turn to the Table of Combinations.
Find page for the combination.

1906

Venus		*Mars*	
Jan 1	Sagittarius	Jan 1—Feb 4	Pisces
Jan 2—Jan 25	Capricorn	Feb 5—Mar 16	Aries
Jan 26—Feb 18	Aquarius	Mar 17—Apr 28	Taurus
Feb 19—Mar 14	Pisces	Apr 29—Jun 11	Gemini
Mar 15—Apr 7	Aries	Jun 12—Jul 27	Cancer
Apr 8—May 1	Taurus	Jul 28—Sep 12	Leo
May 2—May 26	Gemini	Sep 13—Oct 29	Virgo
May 27—Jun 20	Cancer	Oct 30—Dec 16	Libra
Jun 21—Jul 15	Leo	Dec 17—Dec 31	Scorpio
Jul 16—Aug 10	Virgo		
Aug 11—Sep 7	Libra		
Sep 8—Oct 8	Scorpio		
Oct 9—Dec 15	Sagittarius		
Dec 16—Dec 25	Scorpio		
Dec 26—Dec 31	Sagittarius		

Turn to the Table of Combinations.
Find page for the combination.

1907

Venus

Jan 1—Feb 6	Sagittarius
Feb 7—Mar 6	Capricorn
Mar 7—Apr 1	Aquarius
Apr 2—Apr 27	Pisces
Apr 28—May 22	Aries
May 23—Jun 16	Taurus
Jun 17—Jul 10	Gemini
Jul 11—Aug 3	Cancer
Aug 4—Aug 28	Leo
Aug 29—Sep 21	Virgo
Sep 22—Oct 15	Libra
Oct 16—Nov 8	Scorpio
Nov 9—Dec 2	Sagittarius
Dec 3—Dec 26	Capricorn
Dec 27—Dec 31	Aquarius

Mars

Jan 1—Feb 4	Scorpio
Feb 5—Apr 1	Sagittarius
Apr 2—Oct 13	Capricorn
Oct 14—Nov 28	Aquarius
Nov 29—Dec 31	Pisces

Turn to the Table of Combinations.
Find page for the combination.

1908

Venus		*Mars*	
Jan 1—Jan 20	Aquarius	Jan 1—Jan 10	Pisces
Jan 21—Feb 13	Pisces	Jan 11—Feb 22	Aries
Feb 14—Mar 9	Aries	Feb 23—Apr 6	Taurus
Mar 10—Apr 5	Taurus	Apr 7—May 22	Gemini
Apr 6—May 5	Gemini	May 23—Jul 7	Cancer
May 6—Sep 8	Cancer	Jul 8—Aug 23	Leo
Sep 9—Oct 7	Leo	Aug 24—Oct 9	Virgo
Oct 8—Nov 2	Virgo	Oct 10—Nov 25	Libra
Nov 3—Nov 27	Libra	Nov 26—Dec 31	Scorpio
Nov 28—Dec 22	Scorpio		
Dec 23—Dec 31	Sagittarius		

Turn to the Table of Combinations.
Find page for the combination.

1909

Venus

Jan 1—Jan 15	Sagittarius
Jan 16—Feb 8	Capricorn
Feb 9—Mar 3	Aquarius
Mar 4—Mar 28	Pisces
Mar 29—Apr 21	Aries
Apr 22—May 16	Taurus
May 17—Jun 9	Gemini
Jun 10—Jul 4	Cancer
Jul 5—Jul 28	Leo
Jul 29—Aug 22	Virgo
Aug 23—Sep 16	Libra
Sep 17—Oct 11	Scorpio
Oct 12—Nov 6	Sagittarius
Nov 7—Dec 5	Capricorn
Dec 6—Dec 31	Aquarius

Mars

Jan 1—Jan 9	Scorpio
Jan 10—Feb 23	Sagittarius
Feb 24—Apr 9	Capricorn
Apr 10—May 25	Aquarius
May 26—Jul 20	Pisces
Jul 21—Sep 26	Aries
Sep 27—Nov 20	Taurus
Nov 21—Dec 31	Aries

Turn to the Table of Combinations.
Find page for the combination.

1910

Venus

Jan	1—Jan 15	Aquarius
Jan	16—Jan 28	Pisces
Jan	29—Apr 4	Aquarius
Apr	5—May 6	Pisces
May	7—Jun 3	Aries
Jun	4—Jun 29	Taurus
Jun	30—Jul 24	Gemini
Jul	25—Aug 18	Cancer
Aug	19—Sep 12	Leo
Sep	13—Oct 6	Virgo
Oct	7—Oct 30	Libra
Oct	31—Nov 23	Scorpio
Nov	24—Dec 17	Sagittarius
Dec	18—Dec 31	Capricorn

Mars

Jan	1—Jan 22	Aries
Jan	23—Mar 13	Taurus
Mar	14—May 1	Gemini
May	2—Jun 18	Cancer
Jun	19—Aug 5	Leo
Aug	6—Sep 21	Virgo
Sep	22—Nov 6	Libra
Nov	7—Dec 19	Scorpio
Dec	20—Dec 31	Sagittarius

Turn to the Table of Combinations.
Find page for the combination.

1911

Venus

Jan 1—Jan 10	Capricorn
Jan 11—Feb 2	Aquarius
Feb 3—Feb 27	Pisces
Feb 28—Mar 23	Aries
Mar 24—Apr 17	Taurus
Apr 18—May 12	Gemini
May 13—Jun 8	Cancer
Jun 9—Jul 7	Leo
Jul 8—Nov 8	Virgo
Nov 9—Dec 8	Libra
Dec 9—Dec 31	Scorpio

Mars

Jan 1—Jan 31	Sagittarius
Feb 1—Mar 13	Capricorn
Mar 14—Apr 22	Aquarius
Apr 23—Jun 2	Pisces
Jun 3—Jul 15	Aries
Jul 16—Sep 5	Taurus
Sep 6—Nov 29	Gemini
Nov 30—Dec 31	Taurus

Turn to the Table of Combinations.
Find page for the combination.

1912

Venus		*Mars*	
Jan 1—Jan 4	Scorpio	Jan 1—Jan 30	Taurus
Jan 5—Jan 29	Sagittarius	Jan 31—Apr 4	Gemini
Jan 30—Feb 23	Capricorn	Apr 5—May 27	Cancer
Feb 24—Mar 18	Aquarius	May 28—Jul 16	Leo
Mar 19—Apr 12	Pisces	Jul 17—Sep 2	Virgo
Apr 13—May 6	Aries	Sep 3—Oct 17	Libra
May 7—May 31	Taurus	Oct 18—Nov 29	Scorpio
Jun 1—Jun 24	Gemini	Nov 30—Dec 31	Sagittarius
Jun 25—Jul 18	Cancer		
Jul 19—Aug 12	Leo		
Aug 13—Sep 5	Virgo		
Sep 6—Sep 30	Libra		
Sep 31—Oct 24	Scorpio		
Oct 25—Nov 17	Sagittarius		
Nov 18—Dec 12	Capricorn		
Dec 13—Dec 31	Aquarius		

Turn to the Table of Combinations.
Find page for the combination.

1913

Venus

Jan 1—Jan 6   Aquarius

Jan 7—Feb 2   Pisces

Feb 3—Mar 6   Aries

Mar 7—May 1   Taurus

May 2—May 30   Aries

May 31—Jul 7   Taurus

Jul 8—Aug 5   Gemini

Aug 6—Aug 31   Cancer

Sep 1—Sep 26   Leo

Sep 27—Oct 20   Virgo

Oct 21—Nov 13   Libra

Nov 14—Dec 7   Scorpio

Dec 8—Dec 31   Sagittarius

Mars

Jan 1—Jan 10   Sagittarius

Jan 11—Feb 18   Capricorn

Feb 19—Mar 29   Aquarius

Mar 30—May 7   Pisces

May 8—Jun 16   Aries

Jun 17—Jul 28   Taurus

Jul 29—Sep 15   Gemini

Sep 16—Dec 31   Cancer

Turn to the Table of Combinations.
Find page for the combination.

1914

## *Venus*	## *Mars*

Venus		Mars	
Jan 1—Jan 24	Capricorn	Jan 1—May 1	Cancer
Jan 25—Feb 17	Aquarius	May 2—Jun 25	Leo
Feb 18—Mar 13	Pisces	Jun 26—Aug 14	Virgo
Mar 14—Apr 6	Aries	Aug 15—Sep 28	Libra
Apr 7—May 1	Taurus	Sep 29—Nov 10	Scorpio
May 2—May 25	Gemini	Nov 11—Dec 21	Sagittarius
May 26—Jun 19	Cancer	Dec 22—Dec 31	Capricorn
Jun 20—Jul 15	Leo		
Jul 16—Aug 10	Virgo		
Aug 11—Sep 6	Libra		
Sep 7—Oct 9	Scorpio		
Oct 10—Dec 5	Sagittarius		
Dec 6—Dec 30	Scorpio		
Dec 31	Sagittarius		

Turn to the Table of Combinations.
Find page for the combination.

1915

Venus		*Mars*	
Jan 1—Feb 6	Sagittarius	Jan 1—Jan 29	Capricorn
Feb 7—Mar 6	Capricorn	Jan 30—Mar 9	Aquarius
Mar 7—Apr 1	Aquarius	Mar 10—Apr 16	Pisces
Apr 2—Apr 26	Pisces	Apr 17—May 25	Aries
Apr 27—May 21	Aries	May 26—Jul 5	Taurus
May 22—Jun 15	Taurus	Jul 6—Aug 18	Gemini
Jun 16—Jul 10	Gemini	Aug 19—Oct 7	Cancer
Jul 11—Aug 3	Cancer	Oct 8—Dec 31	Leo
Aug 4—Aug 28	Leo		
Aug 29—Sep 21	Virgo		
Sep 22—Oct 15	Libra		
Oct 16—Nov 8	Scorpio		
Nov 9—Dec 2	Sagittarius		
Dec 3—Dec 26	Capricorn		
Dec 27—Dec 31	Aquarius		

Turn to the Table of Combinations.
Find page for the combination.

1916

Venus

Jan 1—Jan 19	Aquarius
Jan 20—Feb 13	Pisces
Feb 14—Mar 9	Aries
Mar 10—Apr 5	Taurus
Apr 6—May 5	Gemini
May 6—Sep 8	Cancer
Sep 9—Oct 7	Leo
Oct 8—Nov 2	Virgo
Nov 3—Nov 27	Libra
Nov 28—Dec 21	Scorpio
Dec 22—Dec 31	Sagittarius

Mars

Jan 1—May 28	Leo
May 29—Jul 22	Virgo
Jul 23—Sep 8	Libra
Sep 9—Oct 21	Scorpio
Oct 22—Dec 1	Sagittarius
Dec 2—Dec 31	Capricorn

Turn to the Table of Combinations.
Find page for the combination.

24

1917

Venus

Jan 1—Jan 14	Sagittarius
Jan 15—Feb 7	Capricorn
Feb 8—Mar 4	Aquarius
Mar 5—Mar 28	Pisces
Mar 29—Apr 21	Aries
Apr 22—May 15	Taurus
May 16—Jun 9	Gemini
Jun 10—Jul 3	Cancer
Jul 4—Jul 28	Leo
Jul 29—Aug 21	Virgo
Aug 22—Sep 16	Libra
Sep 17—Oct 11	Scorpio
Oct 12—Nov 6	Sagittarius
Nov 7—Dec 5	Capricorn
Dec 6—Dec 31	Aquarius

Mars

Jan 1—Jan 9	Capricorn
Jan 10—Feb 16	Aquarius
Feb 17—Mar 26	Pisces
Mar 27—May 4	Aries
May 5—Jun 14	Taurus
Jun 15—Jul 27	Gemini
Jul 28—Sep 11	Cancer
Sep 12—Nov 1	Leo
Nov 2—Dec 31	Virgo

Turn to the Table of Combinations.
Find page for the combination.

1918

Venus		*Mars*	
Jan 1—Apr 5	Aquarius	Jan 1—Jan 10	Virgo
Apr 6—May 6	Pisces	Jan 11—Feb 25	Libra
May 7—Jun 2	Aries	Feb 26—Jun 23	Virgo
Jun 3—Jun 28	Taurus	Jun 24—Aug 16	Libra
Jun 29—Jul 24	Gemini	Aug 17—Sep 30	Scorpio
Jul 25—Aug 18	Cancer	Oct 1—Nov 10	Sagittarius
Aug 19—Sep 11	Leo	Nov 11—Dec 19	Capricorn
Sept 12—Oct 5	Virgo	Dec 20—Dec 31	Aquarius
Oct 6—Oct 29	Libra		
Oct 30—Nov 22	Scorpio		
Nov 23—Dec 16	Sagittarius		
Dec 17—Dec 31	Capricorn		

Turn to the Table of Combinations.
Find page for the combination.

1919

Venus		*Mars*	
Jan 1—Jan 9	Capricorn	Jan 1—Jan 26	Aquarius
Jan 10—Feb 2	Aquarius	Jan 27—Mar 6	Pisces
Feb 3—Feb 26	Pisces	Mar 7—Apr 14	Aries
Feb 27—Mar 22	Aries	Apr 15—May 25	Taurus
Mar 23—Apr 16	Taurus	May 26—Jul 8	Gemini
Apr 17—May 12	Gemini	Jul 9—Aug 22	Cancer
May 13—Jun 7	Cancer	Aug 23—Oct 9	Leo
Jun 8—Jul 7	Leo	Oct 10—Nov 29	Virgo
Jul 8—Nov 8	Virgo	Nov 30—Dec 31	Libra
Nov 9—Dec 8	Libra		
Dec 9—Dec 31	Scorpio		

Turn to the Table of Combinations.
Find page for the combination.

1920

Venus

Jan 1—Jan 3	Scorpio
Jan 4—Jan 28	Sagittarius
Jan 29—Feb 22	Capricorn
Feb 23—Mar 18	Aquarius
Mar 19—Apr 11	Pisces
Apr 12—May 6	Aries
May 7—May 30	Taurus
May 31—Jun 23	Gemini
Jun 24—Jul 18	Cancer
Jul 19—Aug 11	Leo
Aug 12—Sep 4	Virgo
Sep 5—Sep 30	Libra
Sep 31—Oct 23	Scorpio
Oct 24—Nov 17	Sagittarius
Nov 18—Dec 11	Capricorn
Dec 12—Dec 31	Aquarius

Mars

Jan 1—Jan 31	Libra
Feb 1—Apr 23	Scorpio
Apr 24—Jul 10	Libra
Jul 11—Sep 4	Scorpio
Sep 5—Oct 18	Sagittarius
Oct 19—Nov 27	Capricorn
Nov 28—Dec 31	Aquarius

Turn to the Table of Combinations.
Find page for the combination.

1921

Venus

Jan	1—Jan 6	Aquarius
Jan	7—Feb 2	Pisces
Feb	3—Mar 6	Aries
Mar	7—Apr 25	Taurus
Apr	26—Jun 1	Aries
Jun	2—Jul 7	Taurus
Jul	8—Aug 5	Gemini
Aug	6—Aug 31	Cancer
Sep	1—Sep 25	Leo
Sep	26—Oct 20	Virgo
Oct	21—Nov 13	Libra
Nov	14—Dec 7	Scorpio
Dec	8—Dec 31	Sagittarius

Mars

Jan	1—Jan 4	Aquarius
Jan	5—Feb 12	Pisces
Feb	13—Mar 24	Aries
Mar	25—May 5	Taurus
May	6—Jun 18	Gemini
Jun	19—Aug 2	Cancer
Aug	3—Sep 18	Leo
Sep	19—Nov 6	Virgo
Nov	7—Dec 25	Libra
Dec	26—Dec 31	Scorpio

Turn to the Table of Combinations.
Find page for the combination.

1922

Venus		*Mars*	
Jan 1—Jan 24	Capricorn	Jan 1—Feb 18	Scorpio
Jan 25—Feb 16	Aquarius	Feb 19—Sep 13	Sagittarius
Feb 17—Mar 12	Pisces	Sep 14—Oct 30	Capricorn
Mar 13—Apr 6	Aries	Oct 31—Dec 11	Aquarius
Apr 7—Apr 30	Taurus	Dec 12—Dec 31	Pisces
May 1—May 25	Gemini		
May 26—Jun 19	Cancer		
Jun 20—Jul 14	Leo		
Jul 15—Aug 9	Virgo		
Aug 10—Sep 6	Libra		
Sep 7—Oct 10	Scorpio		
Oct 11—Nov 28	Sagittarius		
Nov 29—Dec 31	Scorpio		

Turn to the Table of Combinations.
Find page for the combination.

1923

Venus		*Mars*	
Jan 1	Scorpio	Jan 1—Jan 20	Pisces
Jan 2—Feb 6	Sagittarius	Jan 21—Mar 3	Aries
Feb 7—Mar 5	Capricorn	Mar 4—Apr 15	Taurus
Mar 6—Mar 31	Aquarius	Apr 16—May 30	Gemini
Apr 1—Apr 26	Pisces	May 31—Jul 15	Cancer
Apr 27—May 21	Aries	Jul 16—Aug 31	Leo
May 22—Jun 14	Taurus	Sep 1—Oct 17	Virgo
Jun 15—Jul 9	Gemini	Oct 18—Dec 3	Libra
Jul 10—Aug 3	Cancer	Dec 4—Dec 31	Scorpio
Aug 4—Aug 27	Leo		
Aug 28—Sep 20	Virgo		
Sep 21—Oct 14	Libra		
Oct 15—Nov 7	Scorpio		
Nov 8—Dec 1	Sagittarius		
Dec 2—Dec 25	Capricorn		
Dec 26—Dec 31	Aquarius		

Turn to the Table of Combinations.
Find page for the combination.

1924

Venus

Jan 1—Jan 19	Aquarius
Jan 20—Feb 12	Pisces
Feb 13—Mar 8	Aries
Mar 9—Apr 4	Taurus
Apr 5—May 5	Gemini
May 6—Sep 8	Cancer
Sep 9—Oct 7	Leo
Oct 8—Nov 2	Virgo
Nov 3—Nov 26	Libra
Nov 27—Dec 21	Scorpio
Dec 22—Dec 31	Sagittarius

Mars

Jan 1—Jan 19	Scorpio
Jan 20—Mar 6	Sagittarius
Mar 7—Apr 24	Capricorn
Apr 25—Jun 24	Aquarius
Jun 25—Aug 24	Pisces
Aug 25—Oct 19	Aquarius
Oct 20—Dec 18	Pisces
Dec 19—Dec 31	Aries

Turn to the Table of Combinations.
Find page for the combination.

1925

Venus

Jan 1—Jan 14	Sagittarius
Jan 15—Feb 7	Capricorn
Feb 8—Mar 3	Aquarius
Mar 4—Mar 27	Pisces
Mar 28—Apr 20	Aries
Apr 21—May 15	Taurus
May 16—Jun 8	Gemini
Jun 9—Jul 3	Cancer
Jul 4—Jul 27	Leo
Jul 28—Aug 21	Virgo
Aug 22—Sep 15	Libra
Sep 16—Oct 11	Scorpio
Oct 12—Nov 6	Sagittarius
Nov 7—Dec 5	Capricorn
Dec 6—Dec 31	Aquarius

Mars

Jan 1—Feb 4	Aries
Feb 5—Mar 23	Taurus
Mar 24—May 9	Gemini
May 10—Jun 25	Cancer
Jun 26—Aug 12	Leo
Aug 13—Sep 28	Virgo
Sep 29—Nov 13	Libra
Nov 14—Dec 27	Scorpio
Dec 28—Dec 31	Sagittarius

Turn to the Table of Combinations.
Find page for the combination.

1926

Venus

Jan 1—Apr 5	Aquarius
Apr 6—May 6	Pisces
May 7—Jun 2	Aries
Jun 3—Jun 28	Taurus
Jun 29—Jul 23	Gemini
Jul 24—Aug 17	Cancer
Aug 18—Sep 11	Leo
Sep 12—Oct 5	Virgo
Oct 6—Oct 29	Libra
Oct 30—Nov 22	Scorpio
Nov 23—Dec 16	Sagittarius
Dec 17—Dec 31	Capricorn

Mars

Jan 1—Feb 8	Sagittarius
Feb 9—Mar 22	Capricorn
Mar 23—May 3	Aquarius
May 4—Jun 14	Pisces
Jun 15—Jul 31	Aries
Aug 1—Dec 31	Taurus

Turn to the Table of Combinations.
Find page for the combination.

1927

Venus

Jan 1—Jan 8	Capricorn
Jan 9—Feb 1	Aquarius
Feb 2—Feb 26	Pisces
Feb 27—Mar 22	Aries
Mar 23—Apr 16	Taurus
Apr 17—May 11	Gemini
May 12—Jun 7	Cancer
Jun 8—Jul 7	Leo
Jul 8—Nov 9	Virgo
Nov 10—Dec 8	Libra
Dec 9—Dec 31	Scorpio

Mars

Jan 1—Feb 21	Taurus
Feb 22—Apr 16	Gemini
Apr 17—Jun 5	Cancer
Jun 6—Jul 24	Leo
Jul 25—Sep 10	Virgo
Sep 11—Oct 25	Libra
Oct 26—Dec 7	Scorpio
Dec 8—Dec 31	Sagittarius

Turn to the Table of Combinations.
Find page for the combination.

1928

Venus

Jan 1—Jan 3	Scorpio
Jan 4—Jan 28	Sagittarius
Jan 29—Feb 22	Capricorn
Feb 23—Mar 17	Aquarius
Mar 18—Apr 11	Pisces
Apr 12—May 5	Aries
May 6—May 29	Taurus
May 30—Jun 23	Gemini
Jun 24—Jul 17	Cancer
Jul 18—Aug 11	Leo
Aug 12—Sep 4	Virgo
Sep 5—Sep 28	Libra
Sep 29—Oct 23	Scorpio
Oct 24—Nov 16	Sagittarius
Nov 17—Dec 11	Capricorn
Dec 12—Dec 31	Aquarius

Mars

Jan 1—Jan 18	Sagittarius
Jan 19—Feb 27	Capricorn
Feb 28—Apr 7	Aquarius
Apr 8—May 16	Pisces
May 17—Jun 25	Aries
Jun 26—Aug 8	Taurus
Aug 9—Oct 2	Gemini
Oct 3—Dec 19	Cancer
Dec 20—Dec 31	Gemini

Turn to the Table of Combinations.
Find page for the combination.

1929

Venus

Jan 1—Jan 5	Aquarius
Jan 6—Feb 2	Pisces
Feb 3—Mar 7	Aries
Mar 8—Apr 19	Taurus
Apr 20—Jun 2	Aries
Jun 3—Jul 7	Taurus
Jul 8—Aug 4	Gemini
Aug 5—Aug 30	Cancer
Aug 31—Sep 25	Leo
Sep 26—Oct 19	Virgo
Oct 20—Nov 12	Libra
Nov 13—Dec 6	Scorpio
Dec 7—Dec 30	Sagittarius
Dec 31	Capricorn

Mars

Jan 1—Mar 10	Gemini
Mar 11—May 12	Cancer
May 13—Jul 3	Leo
Jul 4—Aug 21	Virgo
Aug 22—Oct 5	Libra
Oct 6—Nov 18	Scorpio
Nov 19—Dec 28	Sagittarius
Dec 29—Dec 31	Capricorn

Turn to the Table of Combinations.
Find page for the combination.

1930

Venus

Jan 1—Jan 23	Capricorn
Jan 24—Feb 16	Aquarius
Feb 17—Mar 12	Pisces
Mar 13—Apr 5	Aries
Apr 6—Apr 30	Taurus
May 1—May 24	Gemini
May 25—Jun 18	Cancer
Jun 19—Jul 14	Leo
Jul 15—Aug 9	Virgo
Aug 10—Sep 6	Libra
Sep 7—Oct 11	Scorpio
Oct 12—Nov 21	Sagittarius
Nov 22—Dec 31	Scorpio

Mars

Jan 1—Feb 6	Capricorn
Feb 7—Mar 16	Aquarius
Mar 17—Apr 24	Pisces
Apr 25—Jun 2	Aries
Jun 3—Jul 14	Taurus
Jul 15—Aug 27	Gemini
Aug 28—Oct 20	Cancer
Oct 21—Dec 31	Leo

Turn to the Table of Combinations.
Find page for the combination.

1931

Venus

Jan 1—Jan 3	Scorpio
Jan 4—Feb 6	Sagittarius
Feb 7—Mar 5	Capricorn
Mar 6—Mar 31	Aquarius
Apr 1—Apr 25	Pisces
Apr 26—May 20	Aries
May 21—Jun 14	Taurus
Jun 15—Jul 9	Gemini
Jul 10—Aug 2	Cancer
Aug 3—Aug 26	Leo
Aug 27—Sep 20	Virgo
Sep 21—Oct 14	Libra
Oct 15—Nov 7	Scorpio
Nov 8—Dec 1	Sagittarius
Dec 2—Dec 25	Capricorn
Dec 26—Dec 31	Aquarius

Mars

Jan 1—Feb 16	Leo
Feb 17—Mar 29	Cancer
Mar 30—Jun 10	Leo
Jun 11—Aug 1	Virgo
Aug 2—Sep 16	Libra
Sep 17—Oct 30	Scorpio
Oct 31—Dec 9	Sagittarius
Dec 10—Dec 31	Capricorn

Turn to the Table of Combinations.
Find page for the combination.

1932

Venus

Jan 1—Jan 18	Aquarius
Jan 19—Feb 12	Pisces
Feb 13—Mar 8	Aries
Mar 9—Apr 4	Taurus
Apr 5—May 5	Gemini
May 6—Jul 12	Cancer
Jul 13—Jul 27	Gemini
Jul 28—Sep 8	Cancer
Sep 9—Oct 6	Leo
Oct 7—Nov 1	Virgo
Nov 2—Nov 26	Libra
Nov 27—Dec 20	Scorpio
Dec 21—Dec 31	Sagittarius

Mars

Jan 1—Jan 17	Capricorn
Jan 18—Feb 24	Aquarius
Feb 25—Apr 2	Pisces
Apr 3—May 11	Aries
May 12—Jun 21	Taurus
Jun 22—Aug 4	Gemini
Aug 5—Sep 30	Cancer
Oct 1—Nov 13	Leo
Nov 14—Dec 31	Virgo

Turn to the Table of Combinations.
Find page for the combination.

1933

Venus		*Mars*	
Jan 1—Jan 13	Sagittarius	Jan 1—Jul 6	Virgo
Jan 14—Feb 6	Capricorn	Jul 7—Aug 25	Libra
Feb 7—Mar 2	Aquarius	Aug 26—Oct 8	Scorpio
Mar 3—Mar 27	Pisces	Oct 9—Nov 18	Sagittarius
Mar 28—Apr 20	Aries	Nov 19—Dec 27	Capricorn
Apr 21—May 14	Taurus	Dec 28—Dec 31	Aquarius
May 15—Jun 8	Gemini		
Jun 9—Jul 2	Cancer		
Jul 3—Jul 27	Leo		
Jul 28—Aug 21	Virgo		
Aug 22—Sep 15	Libra		
Sep 16—Oct 10	Scorpio		
Oct 11—Nov 6	Sagittarius		
Nov 7—Dec 5	Capricorn		
Dec 6—Dec 31	Aquarius		

Turn to the Table of Combinations.
Find page for the combination.

1934

Venus

Jan 1—Apr 5	Aquarius
Apr 6—May 5	Pisces
May 6—Jun 1	Aries
Jun 2—Jun 27	Taurus
Jun 28—Jul 23	Gemini
Jul 24—Aug 17	Cancer
Aug 18—Sep 10	Leo
Sep 11—Oct 4	Virgo
Oct 5—Oct 28	Libra
Oct 29—Nov 21	Scorpio
Nov 22—Dec 15	Sagittarius
Dec 16—Dec 31	Capricorn

Mars

Jan 1—Feb 3	Aquarius
Feb 4—Mar 13	Pisces
Mar 14—Apr 22	Aries
Apr 23—Jun 2	Taurus
Jun 3—Jul 15	Gemini
Jul 16—Aug 30	Cancer
Aug 31—Oct 17	Leo
Oct 18—Dec 10	Virgo
Dec 11—Dec 31	Libra

Turn to the Table of Combinations.
Find page for the combination.

1935

Venus

Jan 1—Jan 8	Capricorn
Jan 9—Feb 1	Aquarius
Feb 2—Feb 25	Pisces
Feb 26—Mar 21	Aries
Mar 22—Apr 15	Taurus
Apr 16—May 11	Gemini
May 12—Jun 7	Cancer
Jun 8—Jul 7	Leo
Jul 8—Nov 9	Virgo
Nov 10—Dec 8	Libra
Dec 9—Dec 31	Scorpio

Mars

Jan 1—Jul 29	Libra
Jul 30—Sep 16	Scorpio
Sep 17—Oct 28	Sagittarius
Oct 29—Dec 6	Capricorn
Dec 7—Dec 31	Aquarius

Turn to the Table of Combinations.
Find page for the combination.

1936

Venus

Jan 1—Jan 3	Scorpio
Jan 4—Jan 28	Sagittarius
Jan 29—Feb 21	Capricorn
Feb 22—Mar 17	Aquarius
Mar 18—Apr 10	Pisces
Apr 11—May 4	Aries
May 5—May 29	Taurus
May 30—Jun 22	Gemini
Jun 23—Jul 17	Cancer
Jul 18—Aug 10	Leo
Aug 11—Sep 3	Virgo
Sep 4—Sep 28	Libra
Sep 29—Oct 22	Scorpio
Oct 23—Nov 16	Sagittarius
Nov 17—Dec 11	Capricorn
Dec 12—Dec 31	Aquarius

Mars

Jan 1—Jan 14	Aquarius
Jan 15—Feb 21	Pisces
Feb 22—Apr 1	Aries
Apr 2—May 12	Taurus
May 13—Jun 25	Gemini
Jun 26—Aug 9	Cancer
Aug 10—Sep 26	Leo
Sep 27—Nov 14	Virgo
Nov 15—Dec 31	Libra

Turn to the Table of Combinations.
Find page for the combination.

1937

Venus

Jan 1—Jan 5	Aquarius
Jan 6—Feb 1	Pisces
Feb 2—Mar 9	Aries
Mar 10—Apr 13	Taurus
Apr 14—Jun 3	Aries
Jun 4—Jul 7	Taurus
Jul 8—Aug 4	Gemini
Aug 5—Aug 30	Cancer
Aug 31—Sep 24	Leo
Sep 25—Oct 19	Virgo
Oct 20—Nov 12	Libra
Nov 13—Dec 6	Scorpio
Dec 7—Dec 30	Sagittarius
Dec 31	Capricorn

Mars

Jan 1—Jan 5	Libra
Jan 6—Mar 12	Scorpio
Mar 13—May 14	Sagittarius
May 15—Aug 8	Scorpio
Aug 9—Sep 29	Sagittarius
Sep 30—Nov 11	Capricorn
Nov 12—Dec 21	Aquarius
Dec 22—Dec 31	Pisces

Turn to the Table of Combinations.
Find page for the combination.

1938

	Venus		Mars
Jan 1—Jan 22	Capricorn	Jan 1—Jan 30	Pisces
Jan 23—Feb 15	Aquarius	Jan 31—Mar 11	Aries
Feb 16—Mar 11	Pisces	Mar 12—Apr 23	Taurus
Mar 12—Apr 5	Aries	Apr 24—Jun 6	Gemini
Apr 6—Apr 29	Taurus	Jun 7—Jul 22	Cancer
Apr 30—May 24	Gemini	Jul 23—Sep 7	Leo
May 25—Jun 18	Cancer	Sep 8—Oct 24	Virgo
Jun 19—Jul 13	Leo	Oct 25—Dec 11	Libra
Jul 14—Aug 9	Virgo	Dec 12—Dec 31	Scorpio
Aug 10—Sep 6	Libra		
Sep 7—Oct 13	Scorpio		
Oct 14—Nov 15	Sagittarius		
Nov 16—Dec 31	Scorpio		

Turn to the Table of Combinations.
Find page for the combination.

1939

Venus

Jan 1—Jan 4	Scorpio
Jan 5—Feb 5	Sagittarius
Feb 6—Mar 5	Capricorn
Mar 6—Mar 30	Aquarius
Mar 31—Apr 25	Pisces
Apr 26—May 20	Aries
May 21—Jun 13	Taurus
Jun 14—Jul 8	Gemini
Jul 9—Aug 2	Cancer
Aug 3—Aug 26	Leo
Aug 27—Sep 19	Virgo
Sep 20—Oct 13	Libra
Oct 14—Nov 6	Scorpio
Nov 7—Nov 30	Sagittarius
Dec 1—Dec 24	Capricorn
Dec 25—Dec 31	Aquarius

Mars

Jan 1—Jan 28	Scorpio
Jan 29—Mar 20	Sagittarius
Mar 21—May 24	Capricorn
May 25—Jul 21	Aquarius
Jul 22—Sep 23	Capricorn
Sep 24—Nov 19	Aquarius
Nov 20—Dec 31	Pisces

Turn to the Table of Combinations.
Find page for the combination.

1940

Venus		*Mars*	
Jan 1—Jan 18	Aquarius	Jan 1—Jan 3	Pisces
Jan 19—Feb 11	Pisces	Jan 4—Feb 16	Aries
Feb 12—Mar 8	Aries	Feb 17—Apr 1	Taurus
Mar 9—Apr 4	Taurus	Apr 2—May 17	Gemini
Apr 5—May 6	Gemini	May 18—Jul 2	Cancer
May 7—Jul 5	Cancer	Jul 3—Aug 19	Leo
Jul 6—Jul 31	Gemini	Aug 20—Oct 5	Virgo
Aug 1—Sep 8	Cancer	Oct 6—Nov 20	Libra
Sep 9—Oct 6	Leo	Nov 21—Dec 31	Scorpio
Oct 7—Nov 1	Virgo		
Nov 2—Nov 26	Libra		
Nov 27—Dec 20	Scorpio		
Dec 21—Dec 31	Sagittarius		

Turn to the Table of Combinations.
Find page for the combination.

1941

Venus

Jan 1—Jan 13	Sagittarius
Jan 14—Feb 6	Capricorn
Feb 7—Mar 2	Aquarius
Mar 3—Mar 26	Pisces
Mar 27—Apr 19	Aries
Apr 20—May 14	Taurus
May 15—Jun 7	Gemini
Jun 8—Jul 2	Cancer
Jul 3—Jul 26	Leo
Jul 27—Aug 20	Virgo
Aug 21—Sep 14	Libra
Sep 15—Oct 10	Scorpio
Oct 11—Nov 5	Sagittarius
Nov 6—Dec 5	Capricorn
Dec 6—Dec 31	Aquarius

Mars

Jan 1—Jan 4	Scorpio
Jan 5—Feb 17	Sagittarius
Feb 18—Apr 1	Capricorn
Apr 2—May 15	Aquarius
May 16—Jul 1	Pisces
Jul 2—Dec 31	Aries

Turn to the Table of Combinations.
Find page for the combination.

1942

Venus

Jan 1—Apr 6	Aquarius
Apr 7—May 5	Pisces
May 6—Jun 1	Aries
Jun 2—Jun 27	Taurus
Jun 28—Jul 22	Gemini
Jul 23—Aug 16	Cancer
Aug 17—Sep 10	Leo
Sep 11—Oct 4	Virgo
Oct 5—Oct 28	Libra
Oct 29—Nov 21	Scorpio
Nov 22—Dec 15	Sagittarius
Dec 16—Dec 31	Capricorn

Mars

Jan 1—Jan 11	Aries
Jan 12—Mar 6	Taurus
Mar 7—Apr 25	Gemini
Apr 26—Jun 13	Cancer
Jun 14—Jul 31	Leo
Aug 1—Sep 16	Virgo
Sep 17—Nov 1	Libra
Nov 2—Dec 15	Scorpio
Dec 16—Dec 31	Sagittarius

Turn to the Table of Combinations.
Find page for the combination.

1943

Venus

Jan 1—Jan 7	Capricorn
Jan 8—Jan 31	Aquarius
Feb 1—Feb 25	Pisces
Feb 26—Mar 21	Aries
Mar 22—Apr 15	Taurus
Apr 16—May 10	Gemini
May 11—Jun 7	Cancer
Jun 8—Jul 7	Leo
Jul 8—Nov 9	Virgo
Nov 10—Dec 7	Libra
Dec 8—Dec 31	Scorpio

Mars

Jan 1—Jan 26	Sagittarius
Jan 27—Mar 8	Capricorn
Mar 9—Apr 16	Aquarius
Apr 17—May 26	Pisces
May 27—Jul 7	Aries
Jul 8—Aug 23	Taurus
Aug 24—Dec 31	Gemini

Turn to the Table of Combinations.
Find page for the combination.

1944

Venus			*Mars*		
Jan 1—Jan 2	Scorpio		Jan 1—Mar 27	Gemini
Jan 3—Jan 27	Sagittarius		Mar 28—May 22	Cancer
Jan 28—Feb 21	Capricorn		May 23—Jul 11	Leo
Feb 22—Mar 16	Aquarius		Jul 12—Aug 28	Virgo
Mar 17—Apr 10	Pisces		Aug 29—Oct 12	Libra
Apr 11—May 4	Aries		Oct 13—Nov 25	Scorpio
May 5—May 28	Taurus		Nov 26—Dec 31	Sagittarius
May 29—Jun 27	Gemini			
Jun 28—Jul 16	Cancer			
Jul 17—Aug 10	Leo			
Aug 11—Sep 3	Virgo			
Sep 4—Sep 27	Libra			
Sep 28—Oct 22	Scorpio			
Oct 23—Nov 15	Sagittarius			
Nov 16—Dec 9	Capricorn			
Dec 10—Dec 31	Aquarius			

Turn to the Table of Combinations.
Find page for the combination.

1945

Venus

Jan 1—Jan 5	Aquarius
Jan 6—Feb 1	Pisces
Feb 2—Mar 10	Aries
Mar 11—Apr 7	Taurus
Apr 8—Jun 4	Aries
Jun 5—Jul 7	Taurus
Jul 8—Aug 3	Gemini
Aug 4—Aug 30	Cancer
Aug 31—Sep 24	Leo
Sep 25—Oct 18	Virgo
Oct 19—Nov 11	Libra
Nov 12—Dec 5	Scorpio
Dec 6—Dec 29	Sagittarius
Dec 30—Dec 31	Capricorn

Mars

Jan 1—Jan 5	Sagittarius
Jan 6—Feb 13	Capricorn
Feb 14—Mar 24	Aquarius
Mar 25—May 2	Pisces
May 3—Jun 10	Aries
Jun 11—Jul 22	Taurus
Jul 23—Sep 7	Gemini
Sep 8—Nov 11	Cancer
Nov 12—Dec 26	Leo
Dec 27—Dec 31	Cancer

Turn to the Table of Combinations.
Find page for the combination.

1946

Venus

Jan 1—Jan 22	Capricorn
Jan 23—Feb 15	Aquarius
Feb 16—Mar 11	Pisces
Mar 12—Apr 4	Aries
Apr 5—Apr 28	Taurus
Apr 29—May 23	Gemini
May 24—Jun 17	Cancer
Jun 18—Jul 13	Leo
Jul 14—Aug 8	Virgo
Aug 9—Sep 6	Libra
Sep 7—Oct 15	Scorpio
Oct 16—Nov 7	Sagittarius
Nov 8—Dec 31	Scorpio

Mars

Jan 1—Apr 22	Cancer
Apr 23—Jun 19	Leo
Jun 20—Aug 9	Virgo
Aug 10—Sep 24	Libra
Sep 25—Nov 6	Scorpio
Nov 7—Dec 16	Sagittarius
Dec 17—Dec 31	Capricorn

Turn to the Table of Combinations.
Find page for the combination.

1947

Venus

Jan 1—Jan 5	Scorpio
Jan 6—Feb 5	Sagittarius
Feb 6—Mar 4	Capricorn
Mar 5—Mar 30	Aquarius
Mar 31—Apr 24	Pisces
Apr 25—May 19	Aries
May 20—Jun 13	Taurus
Jun 14—Jul 8	Gemini
Jul 9—Aug 1	Cancer
Aug 2—Aug 25	Leo
Aug 26—Sep 18	Virgo
Sep 19—Oct 13	Libra
Oct 14—Nov 6	Scorpio
Nov 7—Nov 30	Sagittarius
Dec 1—Dec 24	Capricorn
Dec 25—Dec 31	Aquarius

Mars

Jan 1—Jan 24	Capricorn
Jan 25—Mar 4	Aquarius
Mar 5—Apr 11	Pisces
Apr 12—May 20	Aries
May 21—Jun 30	Taurus
Jul 1—Aug 13	Gemini
Aug 14—Sep 30	Cancer
Oct 1—Nov 30	Leo
Dec 1—Dec 31	Virgo

Turn to the Table of Combinations.
Find page for the combination.

1948

Venus		*Mars*	
Jan 1—Jan 17	Aquarius	Jan 1—Feb 11	Virgo
Jan 18—Feb 11	Pisces	Feb 12—May 18	Leo
Feb 12—Mar 7	Aries	May 19—Jul 16	Virgo
Mar 8—Apr 3	Taurus	Jul 17—Sep 3	Libra
Apr 4—May 6	Gemini	Sep 4—Oct 16	Scorpio
May 7—Jun 28	Cancer	Oct 17—Nov 26	Sagittarius
Jun 29—Aug 2	Gemini	Nov 27—Dec 31	Capricorn
Aug 3—Sep 8	Cancer		
Sep 9--Oct 6	Leo		
Oct 7—Oct 31	Virgo		
Nov 1—Nov 25	Libra		
Nov 26—Dec 19	Scorpio		
Dec 20—Dec 31	Sagittarius		

Turn to the Table of Combinations.
Find page for the combination.

1949

Venus

Jan 1—Jan 12	Sagittarius
Jan 13—Feb 5	Capricorn
Feb 6—Mar 1	Aquarius
Mar 2—Mar 25	Pisces
Mar 26—Apr 19	Aries
Apr 20—May 13	Taurus
May 14—Jun 6	Gemini
Jun 7—Jul 1	Cancer
Jul 2—Jul 26	Leo
Jul 27—Aug 20	Virgo
Aug 21—Sep 14	Libra
Sep 15—Oct 9	Scorpio
Oct 10—Nov 5	Sagittarius
Nov 6—Dec 5	Capricorn
Dec 6—Dec 31	Aquarius

Mars

Jan 1—Jan 4	Capricorn
Jan 5—Feb 11	Aquarius
Feb 12—Mar 21	Pisces
Mar 22—Apr 29	Aries
Apr 30—Jun 9	Taurus
Jun 10—Jul 22	Gemini
Jul 23—Sep 6	Cancer
Sep 7—Oct 26	Leo
Oct 27—Dec 25	Virgo
Dec 26—Dec 31	Libra

Turn to the Table of Combinations.
Find page for the combination.

1950

	Venus		*Mars*
Jan 1—Apr 6	Aquarius	Jan 1—Mar 28	Libra
Apr 7—May 5	Pisces	Mar 29—Jun 11	Virgo
May 6—Jun 1	Aries	Jun 12—Aug 10	Libra
Jun 2—Jun 26	Taurus	Aug 11—Sep 25	Scorpio
Jun 27—Jul 22	Gemini	Sep 26—Nov 5	Sagittarius
Jul 23—Aug 16	Cancer	Nov 6—Dec 14	Capricorn
Aug 17—Sep 9	Leo	Dec 15—Dec 31	Aquarius
Sep 10—Oct 3	Virgo		
Oct 4—Oct 27	Libra		
Oct 28—Nov 20	Scorpio		
Nov 21—Dec 14	Sagittarius		
Dec 15—Dec 31	Capricorn		

Turn to the Table of Combinations.
Find page for the combination.

1951

Venus

Jan 1—Jan 6	Capricorn
Jan 7—Jan 30	Aquarius
Jan 31—Feb 24	Pisces
Feb 25—Mar 20	Aries
Mar 21—Apr 14	Taurus
Apr 15—May 10	Gemini
May 11—Jun 6	Cancer
Jun 7—Jul 7	Leo
Jul 8—Dec 7	Libra
Dec 8—Dec 31	Scorpio

Mars

Jan 1—Jan 22	Aquarius
Jan 23—Mar 1	Pisces
Mar 2—Apr 9	Aries
Apr 10—May 21	Taurus
May 22—Jul 3	Gemini
Jul 4—Aug 17	Cancer
Aug 18—Oct 4	Leo
Oct 5—Nov 23	Virgo
Nov 24—Dec 31	Libra

Turn to the Table of Combinations.
Find page for the combination.

1952

Venus

Jan 1	Scorpio
Jan 2—Jan 26	Sagittarius
Jan 27—Feb 20	Capricorn
Feb 21—Mar 16	Aquarius
Mar 17—Apr 8	Pisces
Apr 9—May 3	Aries
May 4—May 28	Taurus
May 29—Jun 21	Gemini
Jun 22—Jul 15	Cancer
Jul 16—Aug 8	Leo
Aug 9—Sep 2	Virgo
Sep 3—Sep 26	Libra
Sep 27—Oct 21	Scorpio
Oct 22—Nov 15	Sagittarius
Nov 16—Dec 9	Capricorn
Dec 10—Dec 31	Aquarius

Mars

Jan 1—Jan 19	Libra
Jan 20—Aug 26	Scorpio
Aug 27—Oct 11	Sagittarius
Oct 12—Nov 20	Capricorn
Nov 21—Dec 29	Aquarius
Dec 30—Dec 31	Pisces

Turn to the Table of Combinations.
Find page for the combination.

1953

Venus

Jan 1—Jan 4	Aquarius
Jan 5—Feb 1	Pisces
Feb 2—Mar 14	Aries
Mar 15—Mar 30	Taurus
Mar 31—Jun 4	Aries
Jun 5—Jul 6	Taurus
Jul 7—Aug 3	Gemini
Aug 4—Aug 29	Cancer
Aug 30—Sep 23	Leo
Sep 24—Oct 18	Virgo
Oct 19—Nov 11	Libra
Nov 12—Dec 5	Scorpio
Dec 6—Dec 29	Sagittarius
Dec 30—Dec 31	Capricorn

Mars

Jan 1—Feb 7	Pisces
Feb 8—Mar 19	Aries
Mar 20—Apr 30	Taurus
May 1—Jun 13	Gemini
Jun 14—Jul 29	Cancer
Jul 30—Sep 14	Leo
Sep 15—Nov 1	Virgo
Nov 2—Dec 19	Libra
Dec 20—Dec 31	Scorpio

Turn to the Table of Combinations.
Find page for the combination.

1954

Venus

Jan 1—Jan 21	Capricorn
Jan 22—Feb 14	Aquarius
Feb 15—Mar 10	Pisces
Mar 11—Apr 3	Aries
Apr 4—Apr 28	Taurus
Apr 29—May 23	Gemini
May 24—Jun 17	Cancer
Jun 18—Jul 12	Leo
Jul 13—Aug 8	Virgo
Aug 9—Sep 6	Libra
Sep 7—Oct 22	Scorpio
Oct 23—Oct 26	Sagittarius
Oct 27—Dec 31	Scorpio

Mars

Jan 1—Feb 9	Scorpio
Feb 10—Apr 12	Sagittarius
Apr 13—Jul 2	Capricorn
Jul 3—Aug 23	Sagittarius
Aug 24—Oct 21	Capricorn
Oct 22—Dec 3	Aquarius
Dec 4—Dec 31	Pisces

Turn to the Table of Combinations.
Find page for the combination.

1955

Venus

Jan 1—Jan 5	Scorpio
Jan 6—Feb 5	Sagittarius
Feb 6—Mar 4	Capricorn
Mar 5—Mar 29	Aquarius
Mar 30—Apr 24	Pisces
Apr 25—May 19	Aries
May 20—Jun 12	Taurus
Jun 13—Jul 7	Gemini
Jul 8—Jul 31	Cancer
Aug 1—Aug 25	Leo
Aug 26—Sep 18	Virgo
Sep 19—Oct 12	Libra
Oct 13—Nov 5	Scorpio
Nov 6—Nov 29	Sagittarius
Nov 30—Dec 23	Capricorn
Dec 24—Dec 31	Aquarius

Mars

Jan 1—Jan 14	Pisces
Jan 15—Feb 25	Aries
Feb 26—Apr 10	Taurus
Apr 11—May 25	Gemini
May 26—Jul 10	Cancer
Jul 11—Aug 26	Leo
Aug 27—Oct 12	Virgo
Oct 13—Nov 28	Libra
Nov 29—Dec 31	Scorpio

Turn to the Table of Combinations.
Find page for the combination.

1956

Venus

Jan 1—Jan 17	Aquarius
Jan 18—Feb 10	Pisces
Feb 11—Mar 7	Aries
Mar 8—Apr 3	Taurus
Apr 4—May 7	Gemini
May 8—Jun 22	Cancer
Jun 23—Aug 3	Gemini
Aug 4—Sep 7	Cancer
Sep 8—Oct 5	Leo
Oct 6—Oct 31	Virgo
Nov 1—Nov 25	Libra
Nov 26—Dec 19	Scorpio
Dec 20—Dec 31	Sagittarius

Mars

Jan 1—Jan 13	Scorpio
Jan 14—Feb 28	Sagittarius
Feb 29—Apr 14	Capricorn
Apr 15—Jun 2	Aquarius
Jun 3—Dec 5	Pisces
Dec 6—Dec 31	Aries

Turn to the Table of Combinations.
Find page for the combination.

1957

Venus

Jan 1—Jan 12	Sagittarius
Jan 13—Feb 5	Capricorn
Feb 6—Mar 1	Aquarius
Mar 2—Mar 25	Pisces
Mar 26—Apr 18	Aries
Apr 19—May 12	Taurus
May 13—Jun 6	Gemini
Jun 7—Jul 1	Cancer
Jul 2—Jul 25	Leo
Jul 26—Aug 19	Virgo
Aug 20—Sep 13	Libra
Sep 14—Oct 9	Scorpio
Oct 10—Nov 5	Sagittarius
Nov 6—Dec 6	Capricorn
Dec 7—Dec 31	Aquarius

Mars

Jan 1—Jan 28	Aries
Jan 29—Mar 17	Taurus
Mar 18—May 4	Gemini
May 5—Jun 20	Cancer
Jun 21—Aug 7	Leo
Aug 8—Sep 23	Virgo
Sep 24—Nov 8	Libra
Nov 9—Dec 22	Scorpio
Dec 23—Dec 31	Sagittarius

Turn to the Table of Combinations.
Find page for the combination.

1958

Venus

Jan 1—Apr 6 Aquarius

Apr 7—May 4 Pisces

May 5—May 31 Aries

Jun 1—Jun 26 Taurus

Jun 27—Jul 21 Gemini

Jul 22—Aug 15 Cancer

Aug 16—Sep 9 Leo

Sep 10—Oct 3 Virgo

Oct 4—Oct 27 Libra

Oct 28—Nov 20 Scorpio

Nov 21—Dec 13 Sagittarius

Dec 14—Dec 31 Capricorn

Mars

Jan 1—Feb 3 Sagittarius

Feb 4—Mar 16 Capricorn

Mar 17—Apr 26 Aquarius

Apr 27—Jun 6 Pisces

Jun 7—Jul 20 Aries

Jul 21—Sep 20 Taurus

Sep 21—Oct 28 Gemini

Oct 29—Dec 31 Taurus

Turn to the Table of Combinations.
Find page for the combination.

1959

Venus

Jan 1—Jan 6	Capricorn
Jan 7—Jan 30	Aquarius
Jan 31—Feb 24	Pisces
Feb 25—Mar 20	Aries
Mar 21—Apr 14	Taurus
Apr 15—May 10	Gemini
May 11—Jun 6	Cancer
Jun 7—Jul 8	Leo
Jul 9—Sep 19	Virgo
Sep 20—Sep 24	Leo
Sep 25—Nov 9	Virgo
Nov 10—Dec 7	Libra
Dec 8—Dec 31	Scorpio

Mars

Jan 1—Feb 10	Taurus
Feb 11—Apr 9	Gemini
Apr 10—Jun 1	Cancer
Jun 2—Jul 19	Leo
Jul 20—Sep 5	Virgo
Sep 6—Oct 20	Libra
Oct 21—Dec 3	Scorpio
Dec 4—Dec 31	Sagittarius

Turn to the Table of Combinations.
Find page for the combination.

1960

Venus

Jan 1	Scorpio
Jan 2—Jan 26	Sagittarius
Jan 27—Feb 20	Capricorn
Feb 21—Mar 15	Aquarius
Mar 16—Apr 8	Pisces
Apr 9—May 3	Aries
May 4—May 27	Taurus
May 28—Jun 21	Gemini
Jun 22—Jul 15	Cancer
Jul 16—Aug 8	Leo
Aug 9—Sep 2	Virgo
Sep 3—Sep 26	Libra
Sep 27—Oct 21	Scorpio
Oct 22—Nov 15	Sagittarius
Nov 16—Dec 9	Capricorn
Dec 10—Dec 31	Aquarius

Mars

Jan 1—Jan 13	Sagittarius
Jan 14—Feb 22	Capricorn
Feb 23—Apr 1	Aquarius
Apr 2—May 10	Pisces
May 11—Jun 20	Aries
Jun 21—Aug 1	Taurus
Aug 2—Sep 20	Gemini
Sep 21—Dec 31	Cancer

Turn to the Table of Combinations.
Find page for the combination.

1961

Venus

Jan 1—Jan 4	Aquarius
Jan 5—Feb 1	Pisces
Feb 2—Jun 5	Aries
Jun 6—Jul 6	Taurus
Jul 7—Aug 3	Gemini
Aug 4—Aug 29	Cancer
Aug 30—Sep 23	Leo
Sep 24—Oct 17	Virgo
Oct 18—Nov 10	Libra
Nov 11—Dec 4	Scorpio
Dec 5—Dec 28	Sagittarius
Dec 29—Dec 31	Capricorn

Mars

Jan 1—May 5	Cancer
May 6—Jun 28	Leo
Jun 29—Aug 16	Virgo
Aug 17—Oct 1	Libra
Oct 2—Nov 13	Scorpio
Nov 14—Dec 24	Sagittarius
Dec 25—Dec 31	Capricorn

Turn to the Table of Combinations.
Find page for the combination.

1962

Venus		*Mars*	
Jan 1—Jan 21	Capricorn	Jan 1—Feb 1	Capricorn
Jan 22—Feb 14	Aquarius	Feb 2—Mar 11	Aquarius
Feb 15—Mar 10	Pisces	Mar 12—Apr 19	Pisces
Mar 11—Apr 3	Aries	Apr 20—May 28	Aries
Apr 4—Apr 27	Taurus	May 29—Jul 8	Taurus
Apr 28—May 22	Gemini	Jul 9—Aug 21	Gemini
May 23—Jun 16	Cancer	Aug 22—Oct 11	Cancer
Jun 17—Jul 12	Leo	Oct 12—Dec 31	Leo
Jul 13—Aug 8	Virgo		
Aug 9—Sep 6	Libra		
Sep 7—Dec 31	Scorpio		

Turn to the Table of Combinations.
Find page for the combination.

1963

Venus

Jan 1—Jan 6	Scorpio
Jan 7—Feb 5	Sagittarius
Feb 6—Mar 3	Capricorn
Mar 4—Mar 29	Aquarius
Mar 30—Apr 23	Pisces
Apr 24—May 18	Aries
May 19—Jun 11	Taurus
Jun 12—Jul 6	Gemini
Jul 7—Jul 31	Cancer
Aug 1—Aug 24	Leo
Aug 25—Sep 17	Virgo
Sep 18—Oct 11	Libra
Oct 12—Nov 4	Scorpio
Nov 5—Nov 28	Sagittarius
Nov 29—Dec 23	Capricorn
Dec 24—Dec 31	Aquarius

Mars

Jan 1—Jun 2	Leo
Jun 3—Jul 26	Virgo
Jul 27—Sep 11	Libra
Sep 12—Oct 24	Scorpio
Oct 25—Dec 4	Sagittarius
Dec 5—Dec 31	Capricorn

Turn to the Table of Combinations.
Find page for the combination.

1964

Venus

Jan 1—Jan 16	Aquarius
Jan 17—Feb 9	Pisces
Feb 10—Mar 6	Aries
Mar 7—Apr 3	Taurus
Apr 4—May 8	Gemini
May 9—Jun 16	Cancer
Jun 17—Aug 4	Gemini
Aug 5—Sep 7	Cancer
Sep 8—Oct 4	Leo
Oct 5—Oct 30	Virgo
Oct 31—Nov 24	Libra
Nov 25—Dec 18	Scorpio
Dec 19—Dec 31	Sagittarius

Mars

Jan 1—Jan 12	Capricorn
Jan 13—Feb 19	Aquarius
Feb 20—Mar 28	Pisces
Mar 29—May 6	Aries
May 7—Jun 16	Taurus
Jun 17—Jul 29	Gemini
Jul 30—Sep 14	Cancer
Sep 15—Nov 5	Leo
Nov 6—Dec 31	Virgo

Turn to the Table of Combinations.
Find page for the combination.

1965

Venus

Jan 1—Jan 11	Sagittarius
Jan 12—Feb 4	Capricorn
Feb 5—Feb 28	Aquarius
Mar 1—Mar 24	Pisces
Mar 25—Apr 17	Aries
Apr 18—May 11	Taurus
May 12—Jun 5	Gemini
Jun 6—Jun 30	Cancer
Jul 1—Jul 24	Leo
Jul 25—Aug 18	Virgo
Aug 19—Sep 13	Libra
Sep 14—Oct 8	Scorpio
Oct 9—Nov 5	Sagittarius
Nov 6—Dec 6	Capricorn
Dec 7—Dec 31	Aquarius

Mars

Jan 1—Jun 28	Virgo
Jun 29—Aug 19	Libra
Aug 20—Oct 3	Scorpio
Oct 4—Nov 13	Sagittarius
Nov 14—Dec 22	Capricorn
Dec 23—Dec 31	Aquarius

Turn to the Table of Combinations.
Find page for the combination.

Table of Combinations

The Combinations

Venus in Aries
and
Mars in Aries

ROMANCE

starts quickly. Exact same elements are working. This
one is all brilliant fire: cavalier, magnetic, courageous.
There is balance, direction, confidence, as well as
grace, charm, humor. This one plays to win—and gives
to get. There is nothing small. There is irresistible will.
Romance builds. The beat is powerful. These flames
are fascinating.

LOVE

is *good times*. Affections are intense, emotions are deep.
Idealism propels, optimism adds to the speed,
intelligence gives direction. This one puts it all up—
there is nothing halfway, nothing halfhearted. This one
reaches for love, fights for love.... trumpets blow.
... there is a cavalry charge. It's all high-level, all
noble. This one shapes destiny.

PASSION

is *tremendous*. This one is mental—serves to lavish, to
assure, to nurture. There is volcanic surge—nothing is
denied. It's all well-intentioned, all *ultra*. There is
continuity. Physical exchange is *culmination of love*.

GUIDELINES

You can't get hurt. This combination is stable (one love at
a time). Play this one *long term*.

This combination is in Group **A**.
Turn to page 375.
Italicized words further
explained in the glossary.

Venus in Aries
and
Mars in Taurus

ROMANCE

is *complicated.* High-quality opposite elements are working: brilliant fire and pulsating earth. There is style, grace, magnetism, charm. This one has character—but inner systems are disorganized. This one has difficulty steering, is too quickly inspired, too quickly dedicated. There may be multiple commitments, entanglements, confusion.

LOVE

does better. Affections are generous, emotions are deep. This one lives to love, is equipped to love. There is determination, strength, expanse, depth. Time is the key—it gives this one rhythm. Time settles, gives direction. The longer the relationship, the stronger the relationship. There is great potential. Love can grow, can survive. These grapes can distill to a rare vintage.

PASSION

is *tremendous*. Exotic, pent-up energies are released. This one serves to replenish, to inspire, to nurture. There is an outpouring. This one relates to touch, knows nerve centers. It's all well-intentioned, all high-level. This one reaches for continuity. Physical exchange is *pursuit of fulfillment*.

GUIDELINES

You can't get hurt. This combination is unstable, but there are remarkable compensating attributes. The odds are good to play this one *long term*.

This combination is in Group B.
Turn to page 377.
Italicized words further
explained in the glossary.

Venus in Aries
and
Mars in Gemini

ROMANCE
starts quickly. Combining elements are working: brilliant fire and vital air. This one has flair, confidence, poise, charm. Idealism propels, imagination adds to the speed. This one can steer, is intelligent—can handle romance, can build romance. This one is scintillating. There is a divine spark. This bird flies easily from continent to continent.

LOVE
is *good times.* Affections are evenly released, emotions are regulated. This one is realistic—keeps love together, can cope, can manage. There is nothing maudlin, nothing self-serving. Life is short and talk is cheap, but this one puts it all up. There are shining convictions. Love builds. The beat is exciting. Something sparkles.

PASSION

is *sacred duty*. This one is mental—serves to comfort, to
assure, to inspire. This one responds to need—nothing
is denied. It's all high-level, well-intentioned. There is
continuity. Physical exchange is *expression of faith*.

GUIDELINES

You can't get hurt. This combination is stable (one love at
a time). Play this one *long term*.

This combination is in Group B.
Turn to page 377.
Italicized words further
explained in the glossary.

Venus in Aries
and
Mars in Cancer

ROMANCE

is *complicated*. High-quality opposite elements are working: brilliant fire and pulsating water. There is style, charm, magnetism, grace—but inner systems are disorganized. This one goes in too many directions, is too receptive, too romantic. There may be misplaced sentiment, misunderstandings, entanglements, confusion.

LOVE

does better. Affections are generous, emotions are deep. This one lives to love, thrives on love. Time is the key—it settles, gives direction, enables this one to build. Love can survive and grow. This one has purpose. Time brings a richness: long-awaited rain floods the desert.... the pulse quickens.... there is a dramatic blooming.

PASSION

is *tremendous*. Exotic, pent-up energies are released. This one serves to replenish, to lavish, to nurture. There is awesome surge. This one knows nerve centers. Nothing is denied; it's all high-level, well-intentioned. This one reaches for continuity. Physical exchange is *pursuit of fulfillment*.

GUIDELINES

You can't get hurt. This combination is unstable, but there are remarkable compensating attributes. The odds are good to play this one *long term*.

This combination is in Group B.
Turn to page 377.
Italicized words further
explained in the glossary.

Venus in Aries and Mars in Leo

ROMANCE

starts quickly. Similar elements are working. This one is brilliant nurturing fire, a powerhouse. This one takes care of romance, knows how to keep the thing going. This one is controlled, balanced, mature. There is good will, grace, rhythm. This one is big, strong, honest. Romance is in capable hands. There is understanding. This one is the wood-burning fireplace that warms the house.

LOVE

is *good times*. Affections are rich, emotions are deep. This one has dignity—there is nothing frivolous, nothing stupid. This one has the knack: lives to love, rises to love, can handle love. This one can see, can steer, can cope, can manage. There is spirit, courage, optimism, humor. This one is noble. Love conquers all. There is a radiance.

PASSION

is *sacred duty*. This one is mental—serves to replenish, to assure, to nurture. There is awesome surge. This one responds to need—nothing is denied. It's all high-level. There is continuity. Physical exchange is *culmination of love*.

GUIDELINES

You can't get hurt. This combination is stable (one love at a time). Play this one *long term*.

This combination is in Group **A**.
Turn to page 375.
Italicized words further
explained in the glossary.

Venus in Aries
and
Mars in Virgo

ROMANCE

is *erratic*. Opposite elements are working: scorching fire and barren earth. There is nothing sublime. This one is harsh, dry, puritanical, dense, perverse. There is no intuition, no tact, no humor, no color. Romance can't build—it is without inspiration. This one is nerve-wracking, difficult, frustrating.

LOVE

is *chaotic*. Affections are theatrical, emotions are shallow. This one operates by rote, doesn't know love, can't feed love. This one is without sympathy, without compassion, without warmth. There is nothing lyrical, nothing endearing, no grace. Something is stunted, unawakened. Love can't grow. This one is a small, thin tree with grey leaves.

PASSION

is *tumultuous*. Pent-up energies are released. This one
serves to indulge, to entertain, to ingratiate. This one
knows nerve centers. Nothing is undone. It's all *hyper*,
all confused. Physical exchange is *pursuit of fantasy*.

GUIDELINES

You can get hurt. This combination is unstable. Play this
one *short term*.

This combination is in Group C.
Turn to page 379.
Italicized words further
explained in the glossary.

Venus in Aries
and
Mars in Libra

ROMANCE

starts quickly. Combining elements are working: brilliant fire and perfumed air. There is refinement, control, balance. Idealism propels, imagination adds to the speed. Intelligence gives this one direction— romance builds. There is flair, charm, rhythm, confidence. This one is lyrical. Romance reaches heights. This one is an exotic, graceful bird.

LOVE

is *good times.* Affections are rich, emotions are deep. This one relates to love, knows how to build love, has the knack. There is timing, tact, discretion. This one can see, can steer, can orchestrate. Love takes wing. . . . dreams come true. . . . there is gold at the end of the rainbow.

PASSION

is *tremendous*. This one is mental—serves to assure, to inspire, to nurture. This one is intuitive, knows nerve centers. Nothing is denied. It's all *ultra*. There is continuity. Physical exchange is *culmination of love*.

GUIDELINES

You can't get hurt. This combination is stable (one love at a time). Play this one *long term*.

This combination is in Group A.
Turn to page 375.
Italicized words further
explained in the glossary.

Venus in Aries
and
Mars in Scorpio

ROMANCE

is *erratic*. Opposite elements are working: scorching fire and corrosive water. There are obsessions, extremes, madness. This one makes war, uses romance, conquers to get—is relentless, has no compassion. This one is deceptive and self-serving. There is nothing lyrical. Romance is turbulent. This one is uncivilized.

LOVE

is *chaotic*. Affections are measured, emotions are theatrical. Love is a lure, a tool. This one plays a game, is scheming, callous, driven. This one must feed. Something boils in the blood. There is megalomania. Love can't grow, love is victimized. This one lives in the House of Borgia.

PASSION

is *tumultuous*. Deep, pent-up energies are released. This one serves to indulge, to lavish, to consume. This one sends shivers. The juices flow. There is *uncanny* touch. Nothing is undone, nothing withheld. It's all confused, all *hyper*. Physical exchange is *pursuit of fantasy*.

GUIDELINES

You can get hurt. This combination is unstable. Play this one *short term*.

This combination is in Group C.
Turn to page 379.
Italicized words further
explained in the glossary.

Venus in Aries
and
Mars in Sagittarius

ROMANCE

starts quickly. Similar elements are working. This one is
controlled, low-keyed fire, operates without theatrics.
This one is intelligent, perceptive, capable—copes
easily with tension, has ease of manner, humor, timing.
This one has the knack, knows how to give, knows
when to give. There is poise and confidence. Romance
is in strong hands. This one bends but doesn't break.

LOVE

is good times. Affections are mature, emotions are deep.
There is nothing flamboyant, nothing extravagant.
This one doesn't give roses, doesn't need roses. There is
no ceremony, no pretense, no pressure, no trauma.
Love is togetherness. This one is comfortable,
consistent. There is staying power. Love doesn't
change into hate when the moon is full.

PASSION

is *sacred duty*. This one is mental—serves to support, to assure, to comfort. This one responds to need—nothing is denied. It's all high-level. There is continuity. Physical exchange is *rendezvous with destiny*.

GUIDELINES

You can't get hurt. This combination is stable (one love at a time). Play this one *long term*.

This combination is in Group B.
Turn to page 377.
Italicized words further
explained in the glossary.

Venus in Aries
and
Mars in Capricorn

ROMANCE

is *erratic*. Opposite elements are working: scorching fire and dense earth. There is raw power, wild momentum. Inner systems are disorganized. This one can't see, can't steer, can't cope, can't manage. There is no intuition. This one blunders into romance, gropes at romance. This one is clumsy, forceful, overbearing, primitive. Romance can't build. This one is a charging rogue elephant.

LOVE

is *chaotic*. Affections are theatrical, emotions are eruptive. Impulse propels, recklessness adds to the speed, lack of restraint takes this one too far out. This one is unpredictable. There are collisions, involvements, entanglements. This one is renegade, without grace, without finesse. This one is stupid, self-serving, fatuous, opportunistic. Love can't grow. There is madness.

PASSION

is *tumultuous*. Powerful, pent-up energies are released. This one serves to indulge, to lavish, to consume. There is awesome surge. This one is driven. Nothing is undone, nothing withheld. It's all confused, all *hyper*. Physical exchange is *pursuit of fantasy*.

GUIDELINES

You can get hurt. This combination is unstable. Play this one *short term*.

This combination is in Group C.
Turn to page 379.
Italicized words further
explained in the glossary.

Venus in Aries and Mars in Aquarius

ROMANCE

starts quickly. Combining elements are working: brilliant fire and vibrant air. This one is sociable, spirited, idealistic. There is balance and humor. This one is perceptive, progressive, cosmopolitan, motivated by romance . . . reaches out for romance, can handle romance. This one can see, can steer, can cope, is reliable. There is something sweet. A thoroughbred mare keeps a watchful eye on a newborn colt.

LOVE

is *good times.* Affections flow freely, emotions are deep. This one knows love, knows what love requires, is equal to love. This one is supportive, contributive, intuitive. There is moral strength—nothing frivolous, nothing stupid. This one relates to commitment, is equal to commitment. There is beauty of purpose, shining inspiration. The beat is steady. There is a divine spark.

PASSION

is *sacred duty*. This one is mental—serves to comfort, to assure, to inspire. This one responds to need, rises to need—nothing is denied. It's all high-level, all well-intentioned. There is grace, continuity. Physical exchange is *expression of faith*.

GUIDELINES

You can't get hurt. This combination is stable (one love at a time). Play this one *long term*.

This combination is in Group B.
Turn to page 377.
Italicized words further
explained in the glossary.

Venus in Aries and Mars in Pisces

ROMANCE

is *erratic*. Opposite elements are working: scorching fire and unrestricted water. This one is tossed—can't cope with involvement, can't exist without involvement. There is no direction, no timing, no confidence. This one is vulnerable, pliable, hapless. This one can't manage. Romance can't build; the beat is weak. This one drifts, a ship with no rudder.

LOVE

is *chaotic*. Affections are quick-spilling, emotions are shallow. This one can't handle love, is amateur...gives too much too soon. There is no intuition, no discretion. This one is self-deceptive, too sacrificial, uncertain. There is no judgment. Love can't grow. Unable to find fulfillment, this one spins.

PASSION

is *tumultuous*. Pent-up energies are released. This one serves to indulge, to entertain, to ingratiate. There is permissiveness. This one knows nerve centers, is *uncanny*. Nothing is undone, nothing is withheld. It's all confused, all *hyper*. Physical exchange is *pursuit of fulfillment*.

GUIDELINES

You can get hurt. This combination is unstable. Play this one *short term*.

This combination is in Group C.
Turn to page 379.
Italicized words further
explained in the glossary.

Venus in Taurus and Mars in Aries

ROMANCE

is *complicated*. High-quality opposite elements are working: pulsating earth and brilliant fire. There are courage, chivalry and uncontainable idealism, but inner systems are disorganized. Adventure propels, confidence adds to the speed—but lack of restraint may take this one too far out. This one is too daring, too competitive, too strong. There are instant crusades, instant commitments. There may be entanglements, confusion.

LOVE

does better. Affections are intense, emotions are honest. This one lives to love, loves to love, rises to love . . . but gives too much, wants too much. There are extremes. Time is the key: it softens, gives rhythm. Love can survive, love can grow. It all comes together. The beat is unstoppable. Something towering emerges.

PASSION

is *tremendous*. Exotic, pent-up energies are released. This one serves to comfort, to assure, to nurture. There is awesome surge. Nothing is denied. It's all high-level, all well-intentioned. This one reaches for continuity. Physical exchange is *pursuit of fulfillment*.

GUIDELINES

You can't get hurt. This combination is unstable, but there are remarkable compensating attributes. The odds are good to play this one *long term*.

This combination is in Group B.
Turn to page 377.
Italicized words further
explained in the glossary.

Venus in Taurus
and
Mars in Taurus

ROMANCE

starts slowly. Exact same elements are working. This one is all pulsating earth, magnetic, relates to romance, knows how to build romance. There is intelligence, tact, discretion. This one is capable, has stamina. There is resolve, character—nothing frivolous. Romance has grandeur. There is richness of purpose, grace, charm, rhythm. Something profound emerges. This one is the coming of spring.

LOVE

grows. Affections are dignified, emotions are deep. This one is protective, supportive, compassionate . . . brings conviction to love, brings strength to love, gives something ultimate to love. This one is above doubt, beyond the superficial. This one is enduring. This one is Gibraltar.

PASSION

is *tremendous*. This one communicates by touch—serves to comfort, to replenish, to nurture. This one is intuitive, *uncanny*, knows nerve centers. Nothing is denied. It's all high-level, all *ultra*. There is continuity. Physical exchange is *culmination of love*.

GUIDELINES

You can't get hurt. This combination is stable (one love at a time). Play this one *long term*.

This combination is in Group A.
Turn to page 375.
Italicized words further
explained in the glossary.

Venus in Taurus and Mars in Gemini

ROMANCE

is *erratic*. Opposite elements are working: pulsating earth and restless air. There is charm, humor, a talent to amuse. But the winds blow, inner systems are disorganized. This one is mercurial, whimsical, fickle—there is no balance, no control. This one is unpredictable, propelled by nervous energy. Impulse adds to the speed, lack of restraint takes this one too far out. There are multiple commitments, entanglements. The beat is wild. Romance can't build. There is madness.

LOVE

is *chaotic*. Affections are quick-passing, emotions are shallow. This one is superficial, plays at love, flirts with love, touches just the tip of love. This one doesn't know how to give or how to receive. There is no timing, no rhythm, no intuition. There is something thin, something unlucky. This one is a daisy in December.

PASSION

is *tumultuous*. Pent-up energies are released. This one
serves to indulge, to entertain, to ingratiate. This one is
sporting, there are acrobatics. Nothing is undone. It's
all confused, all *hyper*. Physical exchange is *pursuit of
fulfillment*.

GUIDELINES

You can get hurt. This combination is unstable. Play this
one *short term*.

This combination is in Group C.
Turn to page 379.
Italicized words further
explained in the glossary.

Venus in Taurus
and
Mars in Cancer

ROMANCE

starts slowly. Combining elements are working: pulsating earth and pulsating water. Inner systems are perfectly synchronized and controlled. There is balance, depth, power. This one is determined, has uncanny intuition, knows how to support, when to help. There is superb timing. This one can handle romance, build romance. The beat is strong. There is confidence, rhythm, grace. This one is magical.

LOVE

grows. Affections are rich, emotions are deep. This one is motivated by love, drawn to love, brings splendor to love. This one is honorable, reliable, constant—knows how to feed love, how to protect love—brings religion to love. It's all high-level, devotional. This one is sweet summer rain giving life to green growing things.

PASSION

is *tremendous*. This one communicates by touch—serves to replenish, to comfort, to nurture. This one sends shivers, knows nerve centers. There is a voluptuousness. Nothing is denied, it's all *ultra*. There is continuity. Physical exchange is *culmination of love*.

GUIDELINES

You can't get hurt. This combination is stable (one love at a time). Play this one *long term*.

This combination is in Group A.
Turn to page 375.
Italicized words further
explained in the glossary.

Venus in Taurus
and
Mars in Leo

ROMANCE

is *erratic*. Opposite elements are working: pulsating earth and unrestricted fire. Inner systems are disorganized. This one is too sporting, can't resist adventure. Idealism propels, courage adds to the speed, but lack of judgment brings this one down. This one is too willing, too giving, too impetuous. There is no intuition, no timing, no sense of proportion. The thing spins. Romance can't build. This one is haunted. There is something unlucky.

LOVE

is *chaotic*. Affections are extravagant, emotions are uncontrolled. There are wild aspirations. This one dreams of love, searches for love, is self-deceptive, puts it all in too many places, and can't see, can't steer, can't manage. Love is diluted. There are misplaced loyalties. Love is tossed. There is something vulnerable. This one goes round in circles.

PASSION

is *tumultuous*. Pent-up energies are released. This one serves to assure, to indulge, to nurture. There is unstoppable surge. This one knows nerve centers. Nothing is undone, nothing withheld. It's all *hyper*, all confused. Physical exchange is *pursuit of fulfillment*.

GUIDELINES

You can get hurt. This combination is unstable. Play this one *short term*.

This combination is in Group C.
Turn to page 379.
Italicized words further
explained in the glossary.

Venus in Taurus
and
Mars in Virgo

ROMANCE

starts slowly. Similar elements are working. This one is pulsating receptive earth, organized. There is nothing over-powering, nothing demanding. There is grace, charm, gentility. This one is intelligent, careful, practical, realistic. The lens is clear. There is method, perspective. The pieces must fit. This one knows romance, takes care of romance. The beaver builds the dam.

LOVE

grows. Affections are low-keyed, emotions are deep. There is nothing fickle, nothing superficial. This one is serious, discriminating, moral, reliable. This one relates to love, takes care of love. This one is the capable entrepreneur. The thing builds, the beat is steady, something worthwhile emerges. There is a cottage free from worry or fear.

PASSION

is *tremendous*. This one communicates by touch—serves to replenish, to comfort, to nurture. The senses reel. This one knows nerve centers, is *uncanny*. Nothing is denied, it's all high-level. There is purpose, continuity. Physical exchange is *rendezvous with destiny*.

GUIDELINES

You can't get hurt. This combination is stable (one love at a time). Play this one *long term*.

This combination is in Group B.
Turn to page 377.
Italicized words further
explained in the glossary.

Venus in Taurus
and
Mars in Libra

ROMANCE

is *complicated*. High-quality opposite elements are working: pulsating earth and perfumed air. There is refinement, charm. This one has immense appeal, but inner systems are disorganized. There are extremes. This one is too idealistic, too sporting, too sympathetic, too open, too receptive. This one may be over-involved, over-committed. Romance has difficulty. This one is well-intentioned but may be scattered.

LOVE

does better. Affections are free flowing, emotions are honest. This one is inspired by love, reaches deep for love, flies high for love. Time is the key: it settles, gives rhythm. Confidence grows, the beat slows down, a richness emerges. The longer the thing goes the better. Love builds. There is purpose, substance. Love can survive, dreams come true. This one has character. It all comes together. There is something towering.

PASSION

is *tremendous*. Exotic, pent-up energies are released. This one serves to assure, to indulge, to nurture. This one sends shivers, knows nerve centers. Nothing is denied. It's all high-level. There is dignity. This one reaches for continuity. Physical exchange is *pursuit of fulfillment*.

GUIDELINES

You can't get hurt. This combination is unstable, but there are remarkable compensating attributes. The odds are good to play this one *long term*.

This combination is in Group B.
Turn to page 377.
Italicized words further
explained in the glossary.

Venus in Taurus
and
Mars in Scorpio

ROMANCE

starts slowly. Combining elements are working: pulsating earth and surging water. This one is magnetic, powerful. This one can steer—and drives to something crowning. This one can orchestrate. There is subtle design, velvet vibration, grace, charm. This one is masterful, shapes destiny. The beat is exciting. Romance builds. The pulse quickens. There is wine, there is lovelight.

LOVE

grows. Affections are intense, emotions are deep. There is closeness, blending, belonging. This one is designed for love, can't live without love, keeps love together. This one is irresistible. There is timing, sophistication, intelligence. Love rises, unstoppable. There is rich color, awesome sweep, fulfillment. This one is magical.

PASSION

is *tremendous*. This one communicates by touch—serves to indulge, to lavish, to nurture. This one sends shivers, is intuitive, knows nerve centers. Nothing is denied, it's all *ultra*. There is continuity. Physical exchange is *culmination of love*.

GUIDELINES

You can't get hurt. This combination is stable (one love at a time). Play this one *long term*.

This combination is in Group A.
Turn to page 375.
Italicized words further
explained in the glossary.

Venus in Taurus
and
Mars in Sagittarius

ROMANCE

is *erratic*. Opposite elements are working: pulsating earth and cold fire. Inner systems are disorganized. This one is uncontrolled, impulsive, madcap, frivolous, brazen, high-riding. There are instant involvements, instant entanglements. There is no fear, no restraint. This one is reckless—draws to an inside straight. This one is too nervy, vulnerable to ambush. Romance can't build. This one wears a black sombrero, is unfulfilled, wasted, futile. This one is the fastest, loneliest gun in the west.

LOVE

is *chaotic*. Affections are transitory, emotions are whimsical. This one doesn't know love, can't handle love, doesn't know how to build love. There is something remote. Curiosity propels, restlessness adds to the speed, lack of discretion takes this one too far out. There is nothing abiding, nothing inspirational, no substance. This one is theatrical . . . without character. Something is too wild.

PASSION

is *tumultuous*. Pent-up energies are released. This one serves to indulge, to entertain, to ingratiate—but it's all mechanical. There are no juices. There are acrobatics—nothing is undone, nothing is withheld, but it's all *hyper*, all confused. Physical exchange is *pursuit of fantasy*.

GUIDELINES

You can get hurt. This combination is unstable. Play this one *short term*.

This combination is in Group C.
Turn to page 379.
Italicized words further
explained in the glossary.

Venus in Taurus
and
Mars in Capricorn

ROMANCE

starts slowly. Similar elements are working. This one is pulsating, fertile earth: organized, strong, enduring, practical, efficient, determined. There is depth, balance, direction—nothing impulsive, nothing stupid, no waste of energy. This one relates to romance, knows romance, is designed to build romance. The beat is unstoppable. This one brings something towering to romance, with the character of the oak tree.

LOVE

grows. Affections flow evenly, emotions are constant. This one is motivated by love, has the knack for love. There is timing, tact, intuition. This one knows how to contribute, how to support, knows when to be sympathetic. This one can see, can steer, can cope, can manage—there is control, confidence. Love builds. The thing takes on stature. Two together inspires this one. Two together is an army, all-conquering.

PASSION

is *tremendous*. This one communicates by touch—serves to replenish, to comfort, to nurture. There is awesome surge. This one knows nerve centers, is *uncanny*, sends shivers. Nothing is denied, it's all well-intentioned, all high-level. There is continuity. Physical exchange is *culmination of love*.

GUIDELINES

You can't get hurt. This combination is stable (one love at a time). Play this one *long term*.

This combination is in Group A.
Turn to page 375.
Italicized words further
explained in the glossary.

Venus in Taurus
and
Mars in Aquarius

ROMANCE

is *erratic*. Opposite elements are working: pulsating earth and uncontrolled air. This one is easily influenced, easily fascinated, easily persuaded. This one can't see, can't steer—the lens is blurred. There is self-deception, lack of judgment. This one is too open, too willing, too spontaneous. There is no restraint. Romance can't build. This one spins, is buffeted. A dark cloud overhangs.

LOVE

is *chaotic*. Affections are quick-spilling, emotions are quick-passing. This one is naive, a dreamer, a dupe. Idealism propels, imagination takes this one up, lack of discretion takes this one down. This one can't say no, takes on impossible challenges, goes in too many directions. There are wild flights. This one is vulnerable. There is no timing, no direction. Love can't build, the beat is disjointed. This one is tossed.

PASSION

is *tumultuous*. Pent-up energies are released. This one serves to assure, to entertain, to ingratiate. There are acrobatics. This one knows nerve centers. Nothing is undone, nothing is withheld, but it's all confused, all *hyper*. Physical exchange is *pursuit of fulfillment*.

GUIDELINES

You can get hurt. This combination is unstable. Play this one *short term*.

This combination is in Group C.
Turn to page 379.
Italicized words further
explained in the glossary.

Venus in Taurus
and
Mars in Pisces

ROMANCE

starts slowly. Combining elements are working: pulsating earth and sweet water. Romance is enchanting overture. This one is soft, subtle, modulated. This one operates quietly. There is direction, purpose, nothing frivolous. This one has character. Romance builds. There is charm, grace, something mystical. This one is the North Star at dawn, pale, visible, constant, predictable, reliable.

LOVE

grows. Affections are subdued, emotions are deep. This one lives to love, rises to love, needs to love. Dedication propels, inspiration adds to the speed, intelligence gives balance. This one can cope, can manage. There is tact, discretion, timing, rhythm. This one knows how to build love, how to feed love. The beat is irresistible. There is magic, wine, fulfillment.

PASSION

is *tremendous*. This one communicates by touch, serves to replenish, to comfort, to nurture. This one is intuitive, knows nerve centers. The juices flow . . . nothing is denied. It's all high-level. There is continuity. Physical exchange is *rendezvous with destiny*.

GUIDELINES

You can't get hurt. This combination is stable (one love at a time). Play this one *long term*.

This combination is in Group B.
Turn to page 377.
Italicized words further
explained in the glossary.

Venus in Gemini and Mars in Aries

ROMANCE

starts quickly. Combining elements are working: vibrant air and brilliant fire. This one has spirit, adventure, courage, character, grace, nobility. This one is balanced—has direction and purpose. This one relates to romance, keeps romance going, is capable. There is excitement, something dashing. This one wears a plume, lives in Camelot.

LOVE

is *good times.* Affections flow freely, emotions are deep. There is enthusiasm, optimism, strength, confidence, resolve. This one drives toward fulfillment . . . is equal to love, can handle love. This one can orchestrate. This one is irresistible. There is something towering.

PASSION

is *sacred duty*. This one is mental—serves to support, to assure, to nurture. There is monumental surge. Nothing is denied, it's all *ultra*. There is continuity. Physical exchange is *culmination of love*.

GUIDELINES

You can't get hurt. This combination is stable (one love at a time). Play this one *long term*.

This combination is in Group A.
Turn to page 375.
Italicized words further
explained in the glossary.

Venus in Gemini and Mars in Taurus

ROMANCE

is *erratic*. Opposite elements are working: restless air and receptive earth. This one is uncontrolled—inner systems are disorganized. This one is too quick to give, too willing. Impulse propels, lack of discretion adds to the speed, lack of judgment takes this one too far out. There is no restraint. There are shocks, involvements, entanglements. This one can't steer, can't cope, can't manage. Romance can't build, can't grow. This one is scattered. Rich topsoil is blown away by a frivolous wind.

LOVE

is *chaotic*. Affections are spontaneous, emotions are sincere. This one is amateur. There is no imagination, no strategy, no sophistication. This one is fooled by love, can't handle love, doesn't know how to build love. There is no confidence, no timing, no intuition. This one is vulnerable. Love is tossed. This one is a pretty balloon caught in fickle air currents.

PASSION

is *tumultuous*. Pent-up energies are released. This one serves to indulge, to comfort, to entertain. This one relates to touch, knows nerve centers. There are acrobatics. Nothing is undone, nothing withheld—but it's all *hyper*, all confused. Physical exchange is *pursuit of fulfillment*.

GUIDELINES

You can get hurt. This combination is unstable. Play this one *short term*.

This combination is in Group C.
Turn to page 379.
Italicized words further
explained in the glossary.

Venus in Gemini and Mars in Gemini

ROMANCE

starts quickly. Exact same elements are working. This one is all vital air, idealistic, good-humored, well-intentioned. This one has flair, grace, charm...operates with confidence. There is method. This one sifts relationships, always exploring, experimenting, experiencing. This one is balanced, has direction. This one is nervy, can play the game, relates to romance, is equal to romance. This one is an able ringmaster.

LOVE

is *good times*. Affections are steady, emotions are deep. This one is consistent, controlled, intelligent. This one rises to love, can handle love, relates to commitment. There is nothing overly sentimental, nothing self-deceptive. This one is motivated by two people giving equally, performing equally, exchanging equally. This one is adult, sophisticated...shaping destiny.

PASSION

is *sacred duty*. This one is mental—serves to comfort, to assure, to inspire. This one responds to need, rises to need. Nothing is denied. It's all high-level—there is purpose, continuity. Physical exchange is *expression of faith*.

GUIDELINES

You can't get hurt. This combination is stable (one love at a time). Play this one *long term*.

This combination is in Group B.
Turn to page 377.
Italicized words further
explained in the glossary.

Venus in Gemini
and
Mars in Cancer

ROMANCE

is *erratic*. Opposite elements are working: restless air and dense water. Inner systems are disorganized. There is no confidence. This one must receive more than is given, is romantic but hasn't the knack. There is no rhythm—nothing generous, nothing towering. This one is self-serving, vain, demanding, insecure. This one operates with simple strategies: this for that, two of these for three of those. This one is hard to reach, difficult to convince. Romance can't build. There is tension. This one is frustrating.

LOVE

is *chaotic*. Affections are hesitating, emotions are shallow. This one is too uncertain, has no intuition, commits too late, retreats too soon. This one can't cope, can't anticipate. There is no balance, no conviction, nothing masterful. This one can't handle love, can't support love. This one is buffeted—a quickly disappearing, pale, thin rainbow.

PASSION

is *tumultuous*. Pent-up energies are released. This one serves to indulge, to ingratiate, to nurture. There is an outpouring. This one relates to touch, knows nerve centers, is permissive. Nothing is undone, nothing withheld—but it's all *hyper*, all confused. Physical exchange is *pursuit of fantasy*.

GUIDELINES

You can get hurt. This combination is unstable. Play this one *short term*.

This combination is in Group C.
Turn to page 379.
Italicized words further
explained in the glossary.

Venus in Gemini
and
Mars in Leo

ROMANCE
starts quickly. Combining elements are working: sparkling air and glowing fire. This one has big dreams, is strong. There is courage, direction, balance. There is a certain ease—eyes are clear, palms are dry. There is grace, finesse, humor. This one relates to romance, can handle romance, brings optimism to romance. It's all shining, all warm. There is a divine spark.

LOVE
is *good times*. Affections are rich, emotions are deep. This one is confident, reliable, protective—never petty, never possessive, never demanding. This one handles pressure easily, can cope, can steer, can manage. This one lives to love, can build love, brings magnanimity to love. There is something noble.... The beat is irresistible. Great expectations come true.

PASSION

is *sacred duty*. This one is mental—serves to support, to replenish, to inspire, responds to need. Nothing is denied. It's all with purpose, all high-level. There is continuity. Physical exchange is *expression of faith*.

GUIDELINES

You can't get hurt. This combination is stable (one love at a time). Play this one *long term.*

This combination is in Group B.
Turn to page 377.
Italicized words further
explained in the glossary.

Venus in Gemini
and
Mars in Virgo

ROMANCE

is *erratic*. Opposite elements are working: restless air and barren earth. This one is without force, without depth, without conviction. This one is disorganized, has no balance, no intuition. This one is limited, unsophisticated—easily fascinated, easily persuaded. There are shocks, traps, collisions, catastrophes. This one is too vulnerable, can't handle romance. This one is a rabbit in a snare.

LOVE

is *chaotic*. Affections are frivolous, emotions are shallow. This one is too sympathetic, too willing, too obedient. There are misplaced loyalties, multiple commitments, whimsical crusades. This one is without stature, without vision, self-deceptive. There is confusion...nothing holds together. Love can't sustain. This one is amateur, tossed—just a penny, just a pebble.

PASSION

is *tumultuous*. Pent-up energy is released. This one
serves to lavish, to indulge, to ingratiate. Anything
goes when the whistle blows. This one knows nerve
centers, is *uncanny*. Nothing is undone, nothing
withheld. It's all madness, all *hyper*. There is no
continuity. Physical exchange is *escape from reality*.

GUIDELINES

You can get hurt. This combination is unstable. Play this
one *short term*.

This combination is in Group D.
Turn to page 381.
Italicized words further
explained in the glossary.

Venus in Gemini
and
Mars in Libra

ROMANCE

starts quickly. Similar elements are working. This one is sparkling perfumed air: romance takes wing. There is nothing slow-moving, nothing dull. These winds have color. There is confidence, humor, intelligence, style, charm, rhythm. This one is wide-ranging but selective, idealistic, has character. Romance has meaning. There is magic . . . nightingales sing . . . the pulse quickens.

LOVE

is *good times.* Affections are rich, emotions are deep. This one is controlled, balanced, mature, has substance. There is direction, constancy, gentility, purpose. This one is equal to commitment—love is in capable hands. This one keeps love together, orchestrates. There is sweep to the perspective; the beat is steady. It's all high-level. This one shapes destiny.

PASSION

is *tremendous*. This one is mental—serves to support, to inspire, to nurture. This one sends shivers, knows nerve centers, is intuitive. Nothing is denied. It's all with grace, all *ultra*. There is continuity. Physical exchange is *culmination of love*.

GUIDELINES

You can't get hurt. This combination is stable (one love at a time). Play this one *long term*.

This combination is in Group A.
Turn to page 375.
Italicized words further
explained in the glossary.

Mars in Gemini
and
Mars in Scorpio

ROMANCE
is *erratic*. Opposite elements are working: restless air and unrestricted water. Inner systems are disorganized. Exotic color gives this one allure, magnetism adds to the mystique. This one has dark power, is self-serving. There is guile—a talent to deceive. This one goes in all directions, uses romance, there are hidden motives. The wind carries the song of the siren, the water conceals an undertow.

LOVE
is *chaotic*. Affections are calculated, emotions are primitive. Anticipation propels, lack of restraint adds to the speed. There are extremes, jealousies, possessiveness, tyranny. This one requires total capitulation. Love is war. This one conquers to get...deadly, without feeling. The black widow poised, waiting to spring.

PASSION

is *tumultuous*. Obsessive pent-up energies are released. This one serves to consume, to lavish, to ingratiate. This one relates to touch, knows nerve centers, is intuitive, *uncanny*. Nothing is undone, nothing withheld. It's all madness, all *hyper*, all confused. Physical exchange is *escape from reality*.

GUIDELINES

You can get hurt. This combination is unstable. Play this one *short term*.

This combination is in Group D.
Turn to page 381.
Italicized words further
explained in the glossary.

Venus in Gemini
and
Mars in Sagittarius

ROMANCE
starts quickly. Combining elements are working: vibrant air and controlled fire. There is a solid beat, reliability, idealism, insight. This one is broad-minded, tolerant . . . has grace, rhythm, confidence, character. This one mixes easily but isn't superficial, is speedy but not impulsive, is hard to pin down but meets commitment squarely. This one understands romance, takes care of romance, is a buddy, a pal, a brother, a sister. There is humor, spirit. Something sparkles.

LOVE
is *good times*. Affections are smooth-flowing, emotions are regulated. This one is sure-footed—knows how to build, how to reduce frustration, how to solve problems, how to ease tension. There is a suppleness. This one is cool: there is poise, tact. Love prospers, love grows. There is nothing flamboyant, nothing intense, nothing explosive. Love does well, survives. This one can fly a plane non-stop New York to Paris.

PASSION

is *sacred duty*. This one is mental—serves to assure, to comfort, to inspire. Sensations are delivered to exact requirements. This one responds to need—nothing is denied. It's all well-intentioned. There is continuity. Physical exchange is *expression of faith*.

GUIDELINES

You can't get hurt. This combination is stable (one love at a time). Play this one *long term*.

This combination is in Group B.
Turn to page 377.
Italicized words further
explained in the glossary.

Venus in Gemini
and
Mars in Capricorn

ROMANCE

is *erratic*. Opposite elements are working: restless air and dense earth. Inner systems are disorganized; romance has no meaning. There is intrigue. This one is wayward, deceitful, diabolic, shrewd, calculating, self-serving—operates at a profit. This one doesn't give, has no compassion, no grace. There is nothing lyrical, romance can't build. There is something uncivilized.

LOVE

is *chaotic*. Affections are theatrical, emotions are primitive. This one operates without feeling, without inspiration, without sophistication. Love is without warmth. This one doesn't relate to love, is like a renegade bear—lumbering, domineering, greedy—unimaginative, without charm—a creature of solitude, endlessly roving—dangerous.

PASSION

is *tumultuous*. Obsessive pent-up energies are released. This one serves to consume, to lavish, to ingratiate. There is awesome surge. The method is indelicate. Nothing is undone, nothing is withheld. It's all madness, all *hyper*. There is no continuity. Physical exchange is *escape from reality*.

GUIDELINES

You can get hurt. This combination is unstable. Play this one *short term*.

This combination is in Group D.
Turn to page 381.
Italicized words further
explained in the glossary.

Venus in Gemini
and
Mars in Aquarius

ROMANCE

starts quickly. Similar elements are working: all vital
controlled air. This one aspires, dreams—the spirit is
willing. This one relates to romance, is well-
intentioned, rises to excitement, bends to worthwhile
endeavor. This one is idealistic, has character, nerve,
imagination, conviction, courage. This one relates to
commitment, takes care of romance, builds romance.
This one reaches up to catch a star.

LOVE

is *good times*. Affections are smooth-flowing, emotions
are sincere. There is nothing petty, nothing self-
serving. This one needs to give, needs to build,
measures up to great projects. There is nothing thin,
nothing stupid. This one has timing, poise, direction.
This one can manage, endure. This one takes care of
love, the loyal genie.

PASSION

is *sacred duty*. This one is mental—serves to comfort, to assure, to inspire. This one responds to need, is therapeutic. Nothing is denied. It's all high-level. There is purpose, continuity. Physical exchange is *expression of faith*.

GUIDELINES

You can't get hurt. This combination is stable (one love at a time). Play this one *long term*.

This combination is in Group B.
Turn to page 377.
Italicized words further
explained in the glossary.

Venus in Gemini
and
Mars in Pisces

ROMANCE
is *erratic*. Opposite elements are working: unrestricted
air and uncontrolled water. Inner systems are
disorganized. This one spins. There is no confidence.
This one is susceptible, pliable, impressionable—
without direction, without conviction. This one drifts.
The engine goes, but the propeller is out of the water.

LOVE
is *chaotic*. Affections are quick-spilling, emotions are
maudlin. Impulse propels, lack of discretion adds to the
speed, lack of restraint takes this one too far out. There
are illusions, self-deception, multiple commitments,
entanglements, shocks. This one is amateur...hap-
less...without judgment. This one can't cope with
love. A dark cloud overhangs.

PASSION

is *tumultuous*. Pent-up energies are released. This one
serves to indulge, to entertain, to ingratiate. Anything
goes when the whistle blows. This one knows nerve
centers. There are acrobatics. Nothing is undone,
nothing withheld. It's all madness—all *hyper*, no
continuity. Physical exchange is *escape from reality*.

GUIDELINES

You can get hurt. This combination is unstable. Play this
one *short term*.

This combination is in Group D.
Turn to page 381.
Italicized words further
explained in the glossary.

Venus in Cancer
and
Mars in Aries

ROMANCE

is *complicated*. High-quality opposite elements are working: pulsating water and brilliant fire. There is power, color, richness. This one has character—but inner systems are disorganized. This one can be too noble, too receptive, too idealistic, too romantic. There may be too many crusades, multiple commitments, entanglements, confusion.

LOVE

does better. Affections are fierce, emotions are deep. This one lives to love, charges at love, puts it all up. There is irresistible momentum...the beat is strong. There may be extremes. Time is the key: it mellows, gives this one rhythm. Love can grow, can survive. There is great potential. The longer the thing goes the better. Time gives this one direction. Love builds; there is emergence. The flood subsides, the sun comes out, love conquers all. Life is good.

PASSION

is *tremendous*. Exotic pent-up energies are released. This one serves to support, to replenish, to nurture. There is awesome surge—nothing is denied. It's all high-level, all with purpose. This one reaches for continuity. Physical exchange is *pursuit of fulfillment*.

GUIDELINES

You can't get hurt. This combination is unstable, but there are remarkable compensating attributes. The odds arc good to play this one *long term*.

This combination is in Group B.
Turn to page 377.
Italicized words further
explained in the glossary.

Venus in Cancer
and
Mars in Taurus

ROMANCE

starts slowly. Combining elements are working: pulsating water and pulsating earth. This one is magical—has purpose, quality, depth, grace, charm, sophistication. There is confidence, intuition. This one can cope, can orchestrate. There is nothing frivolous, nothing erratic. Romance unfolds tastefully. This one is designed for romance. There is a royal emergence. Something pulses with promise.

LOVE

grows. Affections are rich, emotions are deep. This one is high-minded; there is courage, compassion. This one is protective, enduring, dedicated, honorable. There is nothing self-serving—love is beyond ego, is sacred. This one brings rare beauty to love. This one is designed for love. There is something sublime. This one has the perfection of Venus de Milo.

PASSION

is tremendous. This one communicates by touch, serves to replenish, to comfort, to nurture. This one knows nerve centers, delivers excellence. Nothing is denied—it's all *ultra*. There is continuity. Physical exchange is *culmination of love.*

GUIDELINES

You can't get hurt. This combination is stable (one love at a time). Play this one *long term*.

This combination is in Group A.
Turn to page 375.
Italicized words further
explained in the glossary.

Venus in Cancer and Mars in Gemini

ROMANCE

is *erratic*. Opposite elements are working: pulsating water and restless air. There is magnetism, charm. Something appeals—but inner systems are disorganized. This one is as elusive as quicksilver. Nervous energy propels, impulse adds to the speed, curiosity takes this one too far out. There are multiple commitments, entanglements, mischief. Romance can't last. This one is a wayward Pied Piper.

LOVE

is *chaotic*. Affections are spontaneous, emotions are uneven. This one loves to love, thrives on love. There are whimsical crusades, wild flights, no balance, no direction, no restraint. Love can't build, can't sustain; nothing holds together. This one is the uncontrolled entrepreneur. Love spins. This one leaves behind a trail of wreckage.

PASSION

is *tumultuous*. Pent-up energies are released. This one serves to indulge, to entertain, to ingratiate. Sensations are delivered sportingly. Nothing is undone, nothing withheld—but it's all *hyper*, all confused. Physical exchange is *pursuit of fulfillment*.

GUIDELINES

You can get hurt. This combination is unstable. Play this one *short term*.

This combination is in Group C.
Turn to page 379.
Italicized words further
explained in the glossary.

Venus in Cancer
and
Mars in Cancer

ROMANCE

starts slowly. Exact same elements are working. This one is all sweet water. There is a richness: velvet receptivity, gentility, grace, control. This one is ultra-sympathetic, ultra-compassionate. There is uncanny intuition. This one can steer, can cope. There is tact, discretion, a knack. This one keeps romance together. The beat is steady, romance builds. The colors are deep, the aroma intoxicating. There is something mystical.

LOVE

grows. Affections are modulated, emotions are devotional. This one is composed—operates quietly, efficiently. This one knows when to give, when to yield. There is finesse, rhythm, timing. This one can orchestrate. There is veiled power, shaping destiny. Love is in good hands. This one brings dignity to love. Something emerges, there is magic, wine, luminescence.

PASSION

is *tremendous*. This one communicates by touch—serves to replenish, to comfort, to nurture. The juices flow, the senses reel. This one knows nerve centers, is *uncanny*. Nothing is denied, it's all *ultra*. There is continuity. Physical exchange is *culmination of love*.

GUIDELINES

You can't get hurt. This combination is stable (one love at a time). Play this one *long term*.

This combination is in Group A.
Turn to page 375.
Italicized words further
explained in the glossary.

Venus in Cancer
and
Mars in Leo

ROMANCE
is *erratic*. Opposite elements are working: pulsating water and uncontainable fire. This one is big, bold, prodigal. This one erupts good-naturedly, but inner systems are disorganized. This one goes in all directions. There is no rhythm, no finesse, no intuition. This one is too fearless, too adventurous, too enthusiastic. There is no restraint—romance can't build, can't sustain. This one is a smoke-blowing, flame-throwing runaway locomotive.

LOVE
is *chaotic*. Affections are spontaneous, emotions are sincere. This one is too quickly ardent, too quickly flowing. Idealism propels, goodwill adds to the speed, lack of intuition takes this one too far out. There is no timing, no discretion. The beat is wild. There are multiple commitments, entanglements. This one can't resist new love, can't turn away from old love. There are upheavals.

PASSION

is *tumultuous*. Pent-up energies are released. This one serves to comfort, to indulge, to inspire. There is awesome surge. This one responds to need. Nothing is undone, nothing is withheld—but it's all *hyper*, all confused. Physical exchange is *pursuit of fulfillment*.

GUIDELINES

You can get hurt. This combination is unstable. Play this one *short term*.

This combination is in Group C.
Turn to page 379.
Italicized words further
explained in the glossary.

Venus in Cancer
and
Mars in Virgo

ROMANCE

starts slowly. Combining elements are working: pulsating water and soft earth. This one operates quietly, with method and intelligence—there is nothing impulsive, nothing scattered. This one can cope, can manage. This one keeps romance together, has the knack. The beat is steady; there is harmony, ease.

LOVE

grows. Affections are modulated, emotions are controlled. This one is reliable, has character, maturity. High-purpose propels, resourcefulness adds to the speed. Uncanny intuition gives direction. This one knows love, knows how to build love, how to sustain love. There is calmness, refinement, rhythm. Roots take hold, the earth opens, seedlings push up, there is greening.

PASSION

is *tremendous*. This one communicates by touch—serves to soothe, to replenish, to nurture. This one understands need, rises to need, knows nerve centers. This one is therapeutic. Nothing is denied—all is with grace. There is continuity. Physical exchange is *expression of faith*.

GUIDELINES

You can't get hurt. This combination is stable (one love at a time). Play this one *long term*.

This combination is in Group B.
Turn to page 377.
Italicized words further
explained in the glossary.

Venus in Cancer
and
Mars in Libra

ROMANCE

is *complicated*. High-quality opposite elements are working: sweet water and perfumed air. There is style, color, charm—but inner systems are disorganized. There are extremes. This one can't resist romance, rises to romance. This one is too chivalrous, too sympathetic. Idealism propels, confidence adds to the speed, vivaciousness takes this one too far out. There may be involvements, entanglements. This one may be over-extended, over-committed; there may be confusion.

LOVE

does better. Affections are extravagant, emotions are sincere, the heart is good. This one can be devotional, loves to love—loves too well. This one is giving. Time is the key: it settles this one. The longer the relationship the better. Time clears the air, gives direction. Love can grow, love can be brilliant. Something towering emerges.

PASSION

is *tremendous*. Exotic pent-up energies are released. This one serves to replenish, to inspire, to nurture. This one relates to touch, knows nerve centers, is intuitive, *uncanny*. Nothing is denied—it's all with grace. There is purpose, a reach for continuity. Physical exchange is *pursuit of fulfillment*.

GUIDELINES

You can't get hurt. This combination is unstable, but there are remarkable compensating attributes. The odds are good to play this one *long term*.

This combination is in Group B.
Turn to page 377.
Italicized words further
explained in the glossary.

Venus in Cancer
and
Mars in Scorpio

ROMANCE
starts slowly. Similar elements are working: pulsating, surging water. This one is magnetic, intense, determined. There is unbending will, character, purpose. There is nothing fickle, nothing scattered. This one relates to romance, feeds on romance, rises to romance, responds to a mystical call. The undaunted, unstoppable salmon swims upstream.

LOVE
grows. Affections are free-flowing, emotions are deep. This one is constant, reliable, protective. There is rhythm, balance, intuition. This one can cope, can steer, can manage—bringing richness and sublime fulfillment to love.

PASSION

is *tremendous*. This one communicates by touch—serves to comfort, to replenish, to nurture. The senses reel. There is a gushing. This one knows nerve centers, is *uncanny*. Nothing is denied—it's all with grace, all *ultra*. There is continuity. Physical exchange is *culmination of love*.

GUIDELINES

You can't get hurt. This combination is stable (one love at a time). Play this one *long term*.

This combination is in Group A.
Turn to page 375.
Italicized words further
explained in the glossary.

Venus in Cancer
and
Mars in Sagittarius

ROMANCE
is *erratic*. Opposite elements are working: pulsating
water and unrestricted fire. Inner systems are
disorganized. This one can't sustain, can't go in a
straight line, can't deal with reality. There are
theatrics, bravado, cockeyed optimism, no sense of
proportion. This one gives too much too soon, requires
too much too soon. There is something contrived,
something doesn't ring true—romance is just a word.
This one plays games.

LOVE
is *chaotic*. Affections are pale, emotions are thin. The
peaks are shallow. Something is just tinsel. Impulse
propels, recklessness adds to the speed, lack of
direction takes this one too far out. There are multiple
commitments, entanglements. This one is too loose,
too wild, too unreliable. Love is just a word. It's all
superficial, all uncontrolled, ill-fated. There is noise
without meaning.

PASSION

is *tumultuous*. Pent-up energies are released. This one serves to indulge, to entertain, to ingratiate. There is an outpouring. This one is sporting. Nothing is undone, nothing withheld—but it's all *hyper*, all confused. Physical exchange is *pursuit of fantasy*.

GUIDELINES

You can get hurt. This combination is unstable. Play this one *short term*.

This combination is in Group C.
Turn to page 379.
Italicized words further
explained in the glossary.

Venus in Cancer
and
Mars in Capricorn

ROMANCE

starts slowly. Combining elements are working:
pulsating water and responsive earth. This one is
balanced, controlled—works at romance, structures
romance—has patience, strength. There is direction,
unstoppable will, power. This one is unflagging. This
one built the pyramids.

LOVE

grows. Affections are free-flowing, emotions are deep.
This one is supportive, protective, compassionate...keeps love together. This one is vigilant,
devotional, reliable. Love is duty. This one is resolute,
can cope, can steer, can orchestrate. Love conquers
all—this one is enduring. The solitary pine still stands
after the avalanche.

PASSION

is *tremendous*. This one communicates by touch—serves to comfort, to replenish, to nurture. There is awesome surge. This one knows nerve centers, is intuitive, *uncanny*. Nothing is denied—it's all *ultra*. There is continuity. Physical exchange is *culmination of love*.

GUIDELINES

You can't get hurt. This combination is stable (one love at a time). Play this one *long term*.

This combination is in Group A.
Turn to page 375.
Italicized words further
explained in the glossary.

Venus in Cancer
and
Mars in Aquarius

ROMANCE

is *erratic*. Opposite elements are working: pulsating water and uncontainable air. This one is well-intentioned, gentle and good-natured, but inner systems are disconnected. This one is easily impressed, easily persuaded—naive, temptable, gullible. Impulse propels, lack of intuition takes this one too far out. There are disappointments. This one can't keep romance together, can't steer, is vulnerable. There are shocks. A bird in a storm flies into high wire.

LOVE

is *chaotic*. Affections are quick-erupting, emotions are quick-passing. This one is amateur . . . too giving or too receptive . . . can't say no, has no strategy, no direction, no timing. This one is bewildered, can't cope. Love doesn't sustain. This one is ineffective. There is a madness. This one pursues windmills.

PASSION

is *tumultuous*. Pent-up energies are released. This one serves to indulge, to comfort, to ingratiate. This one is compliant, delivers sensations sportingly. Nothing is undone, nothing withheld—but it's all *hyper*, all confused. Physical exchange is *pursuit of fulfillment*.

GUIDELINES

You can get hurt. This combination is unstable. Play this one *short term*.

This combination is in Group C.
Turn to page 379.
Italicized words further
explained in the glossary.

Venus in Cancer
and
Mars in Pisces

ROMANCE

starts slowly. Similar elements are working. This one is pulsating sweet water. This one can steer, can cope. There is a sophisticated perspective, an easy style—charm, rhythm, a supple spirit. This one flows with goodwill, humor, sympathy, understanding. This one relates to romance, takes care of romance. A crystal clear spring rises to feed a bubbling brook.

LOVE

grows. Affections are refined, emotions are deep. This one is designed for love. There is nothing fickle, nothing stupid. This one knows how to build, how to give, when to yield. This one has tact—there is timing, finesse, harmony. Love is lush, love is mystical, love has substance. The brook bubbles, a beautiful fish swims, a bird drinks. It's all enchanting. Something sings with fulfillment.

PASSION

is *tremendous*. This one communicates by touch—serves to soothe, to replenish, to nurture. The juices flow. This one is intuitive, knows nerve centers. Nothing is denied—it's all high-level. There is continuity. Physical exchange is *rendezvous with destiny*.

GUIDELINES

You can't get hurt. This combination is stable (one love at a time). Play this one *long term*.

This combination is in Group B.
Turn to page 377.
Italicized words further
explained in the glossary.

Venus in Leo
and
Mars in Aries

ROMANCE

starts quickly. Similar elements are working. This one is
non-scorching pulsating fire—big, brilliant, wholehearted. There is confidence, enthusiasm, aspiration.
Adventure propels, courage adds to the speed, good
intentions add to the flavor. This one is unstoppable:
reaching for romance, rising to romance, feeding on it.
There is a dawning, an emergence. The sun comes up.

LOVE

is *good times*. Affections are ardent, emotions are deep.
This one commits totally—all or nothing at all. This
one gives; there is nothing petty. This one requires
devotion, responds to devotion...is motivated by
love, rises to love...is constant, dedicated, uncompli-
cated. It's all high-level. There is sparkling purpose,
nuclear force. The sun shines brightly.

PASSION

is *sacred duty*. This one is mental—serves to support, to inspire, to nurture. There is awesome surge. Nothing is denied—it's all straight-out release of positive energy, all *ultra*. There is continuity. Physical exchange is *culmination of love*.

GUIDELINES

You can't get hurt. This combination is stable (one love at a time). Play this one *long term*.

This combination is in Group A.
Turn to page 375.
Italicized words further
explained in the glossary.

Venus in Leo
and
Mars in Taurus

ROMANCE

is *erratic*. Opposite elements are working: nurturing fire
and pulsating earth. This one is strong, fearless,
determined. This one has character—but inner systems
are disorganized, without direction, without timing,
without intuition. This one charges into relationships,
commits too soon, pulls up too late. The beat is
uncertain. This one is impetuous, vulnerable. There
are shocks, collisions, entanglements. This one is
drawn to the music but can't dance.

LOVE

is *chaotic*. Affections are extravagant, emotions are
sincere. This one is extreme, but there is something
amateur. This one is too protective, too righteous, too
smothering—gives too much, wants too much: there is
no sense of proportion, no rhythm. This one lives to
love, but can't manage love. The thing spins. This one
can't orchestrate.

PASSION

is *tumultuous*. Deep pent-up energies are released. This one serves to indulge, to comfort, to nurture. This one relates to touch, is *uncanny*, knows nerve centers. Nothing is undone, nothing withheld—but it's all *hyper*, all confused. Physical exchange is *pursuit of fulfillment*.

GUIDELINES

You can get hurt. This combination is unstable. Play this one *short term*.

This combination is in Group C.
Turn to page 379.
Italicized words further
explained in the glossary.

Venus in Leo
and
Mars in Gemini

ROMANCE

starts quickly. Combining elements are working: nurturing fire and vibrant air—romance takes wing. This one is idealistic, balanced, intelligent, graceful. There is charm, rhythm, humor. This one is friendly, giving, inspirational. Something sparkles . . . the spirit soars. This one relates to romance, can handle romance. The heart is good. A bird sings, soft breezes blow, the sun is warm.

LOVE

is *good times.* Affections are refined, emotions flow evenly. This one knows love—can support love, protect love. There is nothing self-serving, nothing erratic. This one keeps the thing going, is sophisticated, can cope. Love is in strong hands. This one is constant, vigilant, protective. It all comes together. This one is the captain of the guard.

PASSION

is *sacred duty*. This one is mental—serves to comfort, to assure, to inspire. This one responds to need. Nothing is denied—it's all high-level. There is purpose, continuity. Physical exchange is *expression of faith*.

GUIDELINES

You can't get hurt. This combination is stable (one love at a time). Play this one *long term*.

This combination is in Group B.
Turn to page 377.
Italicized words further
explained in the glossary.

Venus in Leo
and
Mars in Cancer

ROMANCE

is *erratic*. Opposite elements are working: uncontrolled fire and dense water. Inner systems are disorganized. This one is extreme. Something is muddled—there is no rhythm, no timing. This one gives too much too soon, wants too much too soon, can't play the game. There are instant beginnings, instant endings . . . confusion. This one can't keep it together. A romance is tossed. There are involvements, entanglements. This one goes in circles.

LOVE

is *chaotic*. Affections are unregulated, emotions are self-serving. This one is uncertain, fears humiliation—too turned inward, with imagined injuries, crocodile tears. This one is theatrical, can't manage love, requires too much from love. There is nothing towering, no grace. This one is amateur. There is something unlucky.

PASSION

is *tumultuous*. Deep pent-up energies are released. This one serves to indulge, to comfort, to nurture. This one relates to touch, knows nerve centers. Nothing is undone, nothing withheld—but it's all *hyper*, all confused. Physical exchange is *pursuit of fulfillment*.

GUIDELINES

You can get hurt. This combination is unstable. Play this one *short term*.

This combination is in Group C.
Turn to page 379.
Italicized words further
explained in the glossary.

Venus in Leo
and
Mars in Leo

ROMANCE

starts quickly. Exact same elements are working. This one is all nurturing fire—there is a radiance. This one is honorable, has dignity, is regal. There is strength, courage, timing, the knack. This one is big—has rhythm, humor, intuition, direction. This one brings grace to romance, brings meaning to romance. This one is enduring, with unstoppable conviction. There is shining promise.

LOVE

is *good times*. Affections are wholehearted, emotions are deep. This one is dedicated, compassionate, protective. There is brilliance, purpose. This combination has it all. This one knows how to build, how to contribute, how to support. Love is in strong hands, love conquers all. This one is an unfailing beacon.

PASSION

is *tremendous*. This one is mental—serves to soothe, to inspire, to nurture. Idealism propels, good intentions add to the speed, there is awesome surge. Nothing is denied, it's all *ultra*. There is continuity. Physical exchange is *culmination of love*.

GUIDELINES

You can't get hurt. This combination is stable (one love at a time). Play this one *long term*.

This combination is in Group **A**.
Turn to page 375.
Italicized words further
explained in the glossary.

Venus in Leo
and
Mars in Virgo

ROMANCE

is *erratic*. Opposite elements are working: uncontrolled fire and soft earth. Inner systems are disorganized: there is no rhythm. This one gives too much too soon, is too open, too pliable—too accommodating at the wrong time, too hesitant at the right time. This one can't steer. Comradery propels, good intentions add to the speed, lack of intuition takes this one too far out. There are involvements, entanglements: romance can't build. This one is unlucky. A dark cloud overhangs.

LOVE

is *chaotic*. Affections are muddled, emotions are sincere. There is fear of rejection, dread of humiliation. This one flirts with love, plays at love, is afraid of love . . . has no confidence, no conviction. This one is buffeted. There is something pale. This one is the amateur entrepreneur, spinning.

PASSION

is *tumultuous*. Pent-up energies are released. This one serves to soothe, to indulge, to ingratiate. This one is therapeutic, relates to touch, knows nerve centers. Nothing is undone, nothing withheld—but it's all *hyper*, all confused. Physical exchange is *escape from reality*.

GUIDELINES

You can get hurt. This combination is unstable. Play this one *short term*.

This combination is in Group D.
Turn to page 381.
Italicized words further
explained in the glossary.

Venus in Leo
and
Mars in Libra

ROMANCE

starts quickly. Combining elements are working: vital fire and perfumed air. There is richness. This one is balanced—has direction, dignity, grace, charm, character, humor. There is unending goodwill. This one relates to romance, rises to romance, brings color to romance. There is beauty of spirit, brilliance.

LOVE

is *good times.* Affections are refined, emotions flow evenly. This one knows love, can build love, can manage love—can see, can steer, can anticipate. This one is supportive, contributive, reliable. There is nothing stupid, nothing frivolous. The beat is steady: love grows, love conquers all. This one shapes destiny. This one is a purposeful Pied Piper.

PASSION

is *tremendous*. This one is mental, serves to comfort, to inspire, to nurture. The senses reel. This one knows nerve centers, is *uncanny*. Nothing is denied—it's all *ultra*. There is continuity. Physical exchange is *culmination of love.*

GUIDELINES

You can't get hurt. This combination is stable (one love at a time). Play this one *long term.*

This combination is in Group **A**.
Turn to page 375.
Italicized words further
explained in the glossary.

Venus in Leo
and
Mars in Scorpio

ROMANCE

is *erratic*. Opposite elements are working: nurturing fire and uncontrolled water. This one is fearless, magnetic, has power—but inner systems are disorganized. This one is too forceful, too intense, too wild—obsessed. There is no direction, no balance. Romance is an irresistible game, a narcotic. There is madness in the music. This one can't stop dancing.

LOVE

is *chaotic*. Affections are extravagant, emotions are eruptive. Need for fulfillment propels, lack of discretion adds to the speed, lack of restraint takes this one too far out. This one is extreme: too giving, too demanding, too devotional, too domineering—no rhythm. Love is tossed, love is stormy; there is upheaval. Love can't build. The fires burn, the waters churn, there is scorching steam heat.

PASSION

is *tumultuous*. Deep pent-up energies are released. This one serves to indulge, to lavish, to ingratiate. There is an outpouring. This one knows nerve centers, relates to touch. Nothing is undone, nothing withheld. It's all *hyper*, all confused. Physical exchange is *escape from reality*.

GUIDELINES

You can get hurt. This combination is unstable. Play this one *short term*.

This combination is in Group D.
Turn to page 381.
Italicized words further
explained in the glossary.

Venus in Leo and Mars in Sagittarius

ROMANCE

starts quickly. Similar elements are working: nurturing, low-keyed fire. This one has the knack, can anticipate, can cope, can steer. There is tact, discretion, rhythm, balance, humor. This one is mature, sophisticated. There is something sporting. This one is resilient, has staying power—an able manager. Romance builds, romance is in good hands. This one rides a tireless white horse.

LOVE

is *good times*. Affections are smooth-flowing, emotions are deep. This one can handle love, keeps love together, gets the job done. There is nothing petty, nothing stupid. This one operates without dramatics, without turbulence. This one is ultra-resourceful—reduces pressure, delivers assurance. The beat is steady; love grows. This one knows how to run a railroad.

PASSION

is *sacred duty*. This one is mental, this one serves to soothe, to support, to inspire ... rises to need. There is straight-out release of positive energy. Nothing is denied—it's all high-level. There is purpose, continuity. Physical exchange is *expression of faith*.

GUIDELINES

You can't get hurt. This combination is stable (one love at a time). Play this one *long term*.

This combination is in Group B.
Turn to page 377.
Italicized words further
explained in the glossary.

Venus in Leo
and
Mars in Capricorn

ROMANCE

is *erratic*. Opposite elements are working: uncontrolled fire and dense earth. Inner systems are disorganized. This one is without music, without flair, without humor. This one is narrow, provincial . . . limited, quick-tempered, irritable, unsocial . . . has no rhythm, no direction. This one can't see, can't steer. Romance is tossed, romance is without inspiration. The beat is disjointed. There is turbulence.

LOVE

is *chaotic*. Affections are impetuous, emotions are eruptive. This one is primitive, unequipped—can't sift, can't sort. There is no intuition, no discretion. There are collisions, multiple commitments, entanglements. Love can't build, can't sustain. It's all superficial, all madness.

PASSION

is *tumultuous*. Pent-up energies are released. This one serves to indulge, to entertain, to ingratiate. This one knows nerve centers, relates to touch. Nothing is undone. It's all *hyper*, all confused. There is no continuity. Physical exchange is *escape from reality*.

GUIDELINES

You can get hurt. This combination is unstable. Play this one *short term*.

This combination is in Group D.
Turn to page 381.
Italicized words further
explained in the glossary

Venus in Leo
and
Mars in Aquarius

ROMANCE

starts quickly. Combining elements are working: nurturing fire and vital air. This one is cosmopolitan— liberal, intelligent, organized, balanced—has direction, character. Idealism propels, good will adds to the speed. This one knows how to support romance, how to build romance; there is timing. This one is reliable. The beat is steady. This one is capable: romance is in good hands. There is a talent for doing the right thing.

LOVE

is *good times*. Affections flow easily, emotions are deep. This one gives with grace, receives with grace . . . has tact, discretion, has the knack. This one can steer, can cope, can manage—rises to love, brings shining conviction to love. It's all high level. There is dignity, purpose. This one carries the flame of love gallantly.

PASSION

is *sacred duty*. This one is mental, serves to comfort, to replenish, to inspire. This one knows nerve centers, is therapeutic. Nothing is denied. It's all well-intentioned. There is continuity. Physical exchange is *expression of faith*.

GUIDELINES

You can't get hurt. This combination is stable (one love at a time). Play this one *long term*.

This combination is in Group B.
Turn to page 377.
Italicized words further
explained in the glossary

Venus in Leo
and
Mars in Pisces

ROMANCE

is *erratic*. Opposite elements are working: uncontrolled fire and unrestricted water. Inner systems are disorganized. This one is tossed—weak, impressionable, scattered—without restraint, without judgment. This one is easily fascinated, easily persuaded, easily tempted. There is something sacrificial; there may be masochism. There are involvements, entanglements. This one is drawn to romance, but can't handle romance. There is confusion, madness, futility. This one is a crew with no captain.

LOVE

is *chaotic*. Affections are theatrical, emotions are quick to erupt. There is no intuition. This one can't anticipate, can't cope, can't manage. This one is too giving, too receptive—uncertain, without direction. The beat is wild: love can't build, can't grow. There are catastrophes. A school of minnows swims into the net.

PASSION

is *tumultuous*. Pent-up energies are released. This one serves to indulge, to entertain, to ingratiate. Anything goes when the whistle blows. There is a swooning, the juices flow. This one knows nerve centers—nothing is undone, nothing withheld. This one is virtuoso. It's all *hyper*. There is no continuity. Physical exchange is *escape from reality*.

GUIDELINES

You can get hurt. This combination is unstable. Play this one *short term*.

This combination is in Group D.
Turn to page 381.
Italicized words further
explained in the glossary.

Venus in Virgo and Mars in Aries

ROMANCE

is *erratic*. Opposite elements are working: bland earth and scorching fire. Inner systems are disorganized. There is nothing lyrical—this one is reckless, quick-tempered, overbearing. Impulse propels, ego adds to the speed, lack of restraint takes this one too far out. There are involvements, entanglements. This one is wild—there is upheaval, turbulence. Romance can't build. This one is a flaming comet out of orbit.

LOVE

is *chaotic*. Affections are eruptive, emotions are uncontrolled. This one is difficult to reach, difficult to please. There is no imagination, no humor, no grace. This one handles love explosively, is extreme, is primitive. There is possessiveness, jealousy, flare-ups. Love can't sustain, can't survive. This one is unpredictable, unmanageable. Two comets collide sending fiery debris through the galaxy.

PASSION

is *tumultuous*. Pent-up energies are released. This one serves to lavish, to ingratiate, to conquer. There is no finesse—this one doesn't relate to touch. The action is furious; nothing is withheld. It's all *hyper*, all confused. Physical exchange is *pursuit of fantasy*.

GUIDELINES

You can get hurt. This combination is unstable. Play this one *short term*.

This combination is in Group C.
Turn to page 379.
Italicized words further
explained in the glossary.

Venus in Virgo
and
Mars in Taurus

ROMANCE

starts slowly. Similar elements are working. This one is soft, receptive earth: subtle, sensitive, persevering, enduring. There is nothing reckless, nothing flamboyant. This one keeps romance together—the beat is steady. This one is reliable, intelligent, balanced, controlled, purposeful, determined, ongoing. Romance builds. There is texture, substance, conviction. This one shapes destiny.

LOVE

grows. Affections are finely tuned, emotions are deep. There is sympathy, compassion, ultra-loyalty, stamina. This one is equal to love, weathers storms. This one has courage, character. This one is capable—has the knack. Love picks up momentum, love builds. There is an emergence, a budding, a blooming, a flowering.

PASSION

is *tremendous*. This one communicates by touch, serves to soothe, to replenish, nurture. This one knows nerve centers, is *uncanny*. This one sends shivers. It's all with grace; there is continuity. Physical exchange is *rendezvous with destiny*.

GUIDELINES

You can't get hurt. This combination is stable (one love at a time). Play this one *long term*.

This combination is in Group B.
Turn to page 377.
Italicized words further
explained in the glossary.

Venus in Virgo and Mars in Gemini

ROMANCE

is *erratic*. Opposite elements are working: weak earth and restless air. This one is scattered—wild winds sweep in every direction, the mind takes wing. This one is uncontainable . . . no course is followed. Nervous energy propels, impulse takes this one too far out. This one is inconstant, whimsical, slightly mad. The thing spins. Romance can't build, romance is endless search. This one pursues fantasy.

LOVE

is *chaotic*. Affections are minor flutterings, emotions are thin. This one is indecisive, changeable, cold, remote. There is no direction, no depth, no texture. Love can't sustain, can't build. There is no color, no warmth, no aspiration. This one is frustrating, unrewarding, without character. This one leaves a trail of wreckage.

PASSION

is *tumultuous*. Pent-up energies are released. This one serves to indulge, to entertain, to ingratiate. Anything goes when the whistle blows. This one operates by rote, doesn't care. Nothing is undone. It's all *hyper*, all confused. Physical exchange is *escape from reality*.

GUIDELINES

You can get hurt. This combination is unstable. Play this one *short term*.

This combination is in Group D.
Turn to page 381.
Italicized words further
explained in the glossary.

Venus in Virgo
and
Mars in Cancer

ROMANCE

starts slowly. Similar elements are working: soft earth and pulsating water. This one operates quietly, subtly. This one is no fool, is discreet. This one has poise, taste, charm, grace, dignity. Romance builds—the beat is unstoppable. This one has depth, dimension; romance has meaning. This one is magnetic, mystical, irresistible. Romance conquers darkness. This one is the full moon.

LOVE

grows. Affections are controlled, emotions are deep. This one gets the job done. There is intelligence, understanding, sympathy, compassion. This one has the knack, delivers intensive care. This one can anticipate, can cope—is dedicated, protective, devoted, parental. This one is equal to love, knows love, loves to love, loves to be loved. This one has it all, a jewel.

PASSION

is *tremendous*. This one communicates by touch, serves
to soothe, to indulge, to nurture. The juices flow. This
one knows nerve centers, is *uncanny*. Nothing is denied.
It's all well-intentioned, all high-level. There is
continuity. Physical exchange is *rendezvous with destiny*.

GUIDELINES

You can't get hurt. This combination is stable (one love at
a time). Play this one *long term*.

This combination is in Group B.
Turn to page 377.
Italicized words further
explained in the glossary.

Venus in Virgo
and
Mars in Leo

ROMANCE

is *erratic*. Opposite elements are working: earth and uncontrolled fire. This one is hyperactive, has hyper speed. Inner systems are disorganized; impulse is ruinous. This one is bold, audacious, reckless, without discretion, without intuition. There are extremes. This one goes in too many directions with no restraint. Romance can't take hold, can't build. This one is unmanageable. There is upheaval. This one is nuclear over-spill.

LOVE

is *chaotic*. Affections are theatrical, emotions are eruptive. This one is self-serving, indiscriminate—without regard, without sympathy, without compassion. This one is conceited, arrogant, limited. There is no charm, no humor, no grace. This one can't give, doesn't know how to give . . . love doesn't grow. This one is dense, unrestricted, combustible—dangerous.

PASSION

is *tumultuous*. Pent-up energies are released. This one serves to indulge, to entertain, to ingratiate. Anything goes when the whistle blows. There are acrobatics but no juices; nothing is undone but it's all *hyper*. There is no continuity. Physical exchange is *escape from reality*.

GUIDELINES

You can get hurt. This combination is unstable. Play this one *short term*.

This combination is in Group D.
Turn to page 381.
Italicized words further
explained in the glossary.

Venus in Virgo
and
Mars in Virgo

ROMANCE

starts slowly. Exact same elements are working. This one is all soft earth: controlled, balanced, serious, efficient, precise. There is nothing extravagant, nothing extroverted. This one is organized, takes care of romance, has character and patience. Romance is in good hands. There are no theatrics, no waste of energy. This one deals with reality.

LOVE

grows. Affections are sub-surface, emotions are rarely displayed. This one delivers services—a professional. This one can't feel love: there is something bloodless. But this one can handle love, can cope, can anticipate, can manage. This one keeps love together. Love is duty, and this one rises to duty. Love builds. This one gets the job done.

PASSION

is *tremendous*. This one communicates by touch, serves to indulge, to replenish, to inspire. This one is intuitive, knows nerve centers, responds to need. Nothing is denied. It's all high-level. There is purpose, continuity. Physical exchange is *expression of faith*.

GUIDELINES

You can't get hurt. This combination is stable (one love at a time). Play this one *long term*.

This combination is in Group B.
Turn to page 377.
Italicized words further
explained in the glossary.

Venus in Virgo
and
Mars in Libra

ROMANCE

is *erratic*. Opposite elements are working: barren earth and perfumed air. There is style, but inner systems are disorganized. This one is impulsive, quickly fascinated, rash, ardent—without balance, without control. There is something driven. There are involvements, entanglements. Romance can't build, can't cope. There is a fine line between madness and inspiration.

LOVE

is *chaotic*. Affections are eruptive, emotions are sincere. This one is responsive to love, inspired by love, motivated by love. This one is well-intentioned, has character, but is caught in the switches. This one can't say "No" to old love, can't say "No" to new love. There is ongoing turmoil, misplaced loyalty—confusion. This one can't stop dancing.

PASSION

is *tumultuous*. Pent-up energies are released. This one serves to indulge, to inspire, to nurture. There is an outpouring. This one knows nerve centers. Nothing is undone, nothing withheld. It's all *hyper*. This one tries for continuity but can't achieve it. Physical exchange is *pursuit of fulfillment*.

GUIDELINES

You can get hurt. This combination is unstable. Play this one *short term*.

This combination is in Group C.
Turn to page 379.
Italicized words further
explained in the glossary.

Venus in Virgo
and
Mars in Scorpio

ROMANCE

starts slowly. Combining elements are working: soft earth and surging water. There is magnetism, unstoppable will, control. Inner mechanisms run smoothly. This one can steer, has great perception. This one can anticipate, can cope, can orchestrate. Romance builds—the beat is steady. There is conviction, determination. This one has depth— romance has quality. This one shapes destiny.

LOVE

grows. Affections are regulated, emotions are deep. This one keeps it together: is protective, supportive, enduring. There is rhythm, grace, sophistication, capability. Love builds. This one operates on a watery plane—there is a swelling, a rising, a cresting. Love rides the flood tide. There is something irresistible.

PASSION

is *tremendous*. This one communicates by touch, serves to comfort, to replenish, to nurture. This one is intuitive, knows nerve centers, is *uncanny*. Nothing is denied. It's all high-level; there is purpose, continuity. Physical exchange is *rendezvous with destiny*.

GUIDELINES

You can't get hurt. This combination is stable (one love at a time). Play this one *long term*.

This combination is in Group B.
Turn to page 377.
Italicized words further
explained in the glossary.

Venus in Virgo
and
Mars in Sagittarius

ROMANCE

is *erratic*. Opposite elements are working: barren earth
and unrestricted fire. Inner systems are disorganized.
This one is disjointed, disconnected, without rhythm,
without timing, unpredictable, scattered, too ex-
tended, too adventurous. There are shocks, collisions,
involvements, entanglements. This one is driven, there
is something madcap, the beat is frenzied. Romance
can't build. This one stays too long at the wrong
parties.

LOVE

is *chaotic*. Affections are without warmth, emotions are
without depth. Commitments have no meaning—it's
all games, maneuvers, empty encounters. This one is
unmanageable, unbridled, uncaring. This one doesn't
relate to love, has no interest in love. This one flies a
colorless flag.

PASSION

is *tumultuous*. Pent-up energy is released. This one serves to indulge, to entertain, to ingratiate. Anything goes when the whistle blows, but there is no inspiration. This one doesn't relate to need. There are acrobatics, nothing is withheld, it's all *hyper*. There is no continuity. Physical exchange is *escape from reality*.

GUIDELINES

You can get hurt. This combination is unstable. Play this one *short term*.

This combination is in Group D.
Turn to page 381.
Italicized words further
explained in the glossary.

Venus in Virgo
and
Mars in Capricorn

ROMANCE

starts slowly. Similar elements are working. This one is soft receptive earth. There is balance, depth, strength, determination, character. Inner systems are organized. This one has tact, discretion, a sense of order—the perception is clear. This one does the necessary, is practical, reliable, a caretaker. Romance takes hold, romance builds. There is something abiding, something selfless. There is a shine in the eyes of the faithful collie.

LOVE

grows. Affections are evenly released, emotions are sincere. There is nothing shallow, nothing stupid. This one is warm, protective, giving—can cope, communicate assurance and understanding, reduce pressure, cut through confusion. This one has the knack. There is humor—and a talent for simple solutions. This one is easy on the nerves, has rhythm. Love is in good hands. The beat is steady: love builds, love sustains. This one is comfortable.

PASSION

is *tremendous*. This one communicates by touch, serves to soothe, to comfort, to replenish. This one is intuitive, knows nerve centers, is *uncanny*. Nothing is denied. It's all well-intentioned. There is continuity. Physical exchange is *expression of faith*.

GUIDELINES

You can't get hurt. This combination is stable (one love at a time). Play this one *long term*.

This combination is in Group B.
Turn to page 377.
Italicized words further
explained in the glossary.

Venus in Virgo
and
Mars in Aquarius

ROMANCE

is *erratic*. Opposite elements are working: weak earth and uncontainable air. There is goodwill. This one is humane—but inner systems are disorganized. This one can't play the game, is too sincere, too believing—too receptive, impressionable, naive, tossed. There are misplaced loyalties, multiple commitments, entanglements. This one is scattered...there is confusion...romance can't build. This one lives in a house of straw.

LOVE

is *chaotic*. Affections are quickly aroused, emotions are quickly dedicated. This one is too open, too outgoing. Idealism propels, impulse adds to the speed, lack of judgment takes this one too far out. There is no intuition, no direction. This one can't see, can't steer. There are dead ends, traps, shocks, disillusionments. This one can't find love, is unlucky. A pigeon catches the eye of a falcon.

PASSION

is *tumultuous*. This one is mental. Pent-up energies are released. This one serves to indulge, to inspire, to ingratiate. Anything goes when the whistle blows. This one is permissive. Nothing is undone, nothing withheld. It's all *hyper*. There is no continuity. Physical exchange is *escape from reality*.

GUIDELINES

You can get hurt. This combination is unstable. Play this one *short term*.

This combination is in Group D.
Turn to page 381.
Italicized words further
explained in the glossary.

Venus in Virgo and Mars in Pisces

ROMANCE

starts slowly. Combining elements are working: soft earth and sweet water. This one has taste, modesty, refinement ... discretion, balance, honor ... insight, clear perspectives. This one knows life is full of shocks, knows life is unpredictable. This one can cope—is supportive, sympathetic, loyal, saintly, purposeful. Romance is in good hands, romance builds. There is great promise. This one shapes destiny.

LOVE

grows. Affections are smooth-flowing, emotions are deep. This one is dedicated, radiates regard, delivers assurance. This one is yielding, receptive, reliable. There is quiet efficiency. This one is the intelligent entrepreneur—takes care of love, keeps love together, is devotional. This one has the knack. Green growing things open to warm gentle summer rain.

PASSION

is *tremendous*. This one communicates by touch, serves to soothe, to replenish, to nurture. This one sends shivers, knows nerve centers, is intuitive, *uncanny*. Nothing is denied. It's all well-intentioned. There is continuity. Physical exchange is *rendezvous with destiny*.

GUIDELINES

You can't get hurt. This combination is stable (one love at a time). Play this one *long term*.

This combination is in Group B.
Turn to page 377.
Italicized words further
explained in the glossary.

Venus in Libra and Mars in Aries

ROMANCE

starts quickly. Combining elements are working: perfumed air and brilliant fire. This one has momentum, courage, confidence—and flair. This one is gallant, big. There is idealism, imagination, humor, something cavalier. This one is motivated by romance, rises to romance. This one rides a winged chariot.

LOVE

is *good times.* Affections are outgoing, emotions are constant. This one gives, is protective, delivers strength, is dynamic. There is unstoppable spirit, unstoppable enthusiasm. The beat is exciting. This one is noble, majestic—bringing quality to love, something towering to love. This one is the defender of the right.

PASSION

is *sacred duty*. This one is mental, serves to support, to inspire, to nurture. This one responds to need, rises to need. There is straight-out release of positive energy. Nothing is denied, it's all *ultra*. There is continuity. Physical exchange is *culmination of love*.

GUIDELINES

You can't get hurt. This combination is stable (one love at a time). Play this one *long term*.

This combination is in Group A.
Turn to page 375.
Italicized words further
explained in the glossary.

Venus in Libra and Mars in Taurus

ROMANCE

is *complicated*. High-quality opposite elements are working: perfumed air and pulsating earth—magnetic, powerful, colorful. Inner systems are disorganized. This one is extreme: no rhythm, no timing. This one gives too much or too little, is instantly dedicated or instantly unreachable. There is nothing supple. This one can't play the game, has no finesse. This one can't handle romance, is mystified by romance. There may be involvements, entanglements, confusion.

LOVE

does better. Affections are extravagant, emotions are sincere. Time is the key: time allows this one to focus—gives foundation, direction. The longer the relationship the better. There is an emergence . . . love builds, confidence grows. There is an ascent, the thing takes on stature, love survives. A gentle sensitive wind carries seed to rich incubative earth.

PASSION

is *tremendous*. This one communicates by touch, serves to soothe, to replenish, to nurture. This one is intuitive, uncanny, knows nerve centers. Nothing is denied; it's all with purpose. This one reaches for continuity. Physical exchange is *pursuit of fulfillment*.

GUIDELINES

You can't get hurt. This combination is unstable—but there are remarkable compensating attributes. The odds are good to play this one *long term*.

This combination is in Group B.
Turn to page 377.
Italicized words further
explained in the glossary.

Venus in Libra and Mars in Gemini

ROMANCE

starts quickly. Similar elements are working. This one is perfumed vital air. The style is easy—there is finesse, charm. This one is clear-sighted, balanced, controlled. Idealism propels, imagination adds to the speed, intelligence adds to the direction, humor adds to the flavor. This one has it all, can handle romance, rises to romance, comes alive with romance. Something sparkles. This one flies high.

LOVE

is *good times.* Affections are modulated, emotions flow smoothly. This one is the capable entrepreneur: efficient, resourceful, reliable. This one can see, can steer, can cope. There is nothing frivolous, nothing self-serving. Love is in good hands . . . love builds. This one is a rare sweet-singing bird taking care of the nest.

PASSION

is *sacred duty*. This one is mental, serves to support, to assure, to inspire. This one responds to need; nothing is denied. It's all well-intentioned. There is something *ultra*, there is continuity. Physical exchange is *expression of faith*.

GUIDELINES

You can't get hurt. This combination is stable (one love at a time). Play this one *long term*.

This combination is in Group A.
Turn to page 375.
Italicized words further
explained in the glossary.

Venus in Libra and Mars in Cancer

ROMANCE

is *complicated*. High-quality opposite elements are working: perfumed air and pulsating water. This one is magnetic, colorful, charming—but inner systems are disorganized. This one is too receptive, too sympathetic, goes in too many directions. There are multiple commitments, entanglements. There is too much sentiment for the wrong relationship, too little confidence for the right relationship. This one has difficulty with romance. There may be confusion.

LOVE

does better. Affections are extravagant, emotions are sincere. This one keeps a contract—there is richness of intent. This one lives for love, can be devotional. Time is the key: time settles this one, gives clear focus. Something distills. The longer the thing goes the stronger it is. This one has potential. Love can survive. The winds subside, the tides subside. A hauntingly beautiful full moon rises.

PASSION

is *tremendous*. Exotic pent-up energies are released. This one serves to assure, to comfort, to nurture. This one relates to touch, is intuitive. Nothing is denied. It's all high-level, something *ultra*. This one reaches for continuity. Physical exchange is *pursuit of fulfillment*.

GUIDELINES

You can't get hurt. This combination is unstable—but there are remarkable compensating attributes. Odds are good to play this one *long term*.

This combination is in Group B.
Turn to page 377.
Italicized words further
explained in the glossary.

Venus in Libra and Mars in Leo

ROMANCE

starts quickly. Combining elements are working: vital air and brilliant fire. This one is loyal, chivalrous, honorable, courageous... tolerant, liberal, compassionate. There is towering conviction. This one gives beyond giving, stands to be counted. There is noblesse oblige, style, grace, humor. Romance romps, romance sparkles. The plume is held high, the spirit soars.

LOVE

is *good times*. Affections are warm, emotions are deep. This one is parental: protective, supportive, patient, strong. This one is intelligent, can cope, can steer. This one is the efficient, benevolent entrepreneur. Love is in good hands, love grows, the beat is strong. There is glory. Love conquers darkness. This one is a citadel of devotion.

PASSION

is *tremendous*. This one is mental, serves to comfort, to inspire, to nurture. There is awesome surge; nothing is denied. There is straight-out release of positive energy. It's all *ultra*. There is continuity. Physical exchange is *culmination of love*.

GUIDELINES

You can't get hurt. This combination is stable (one love at a time). Play this one *long term*.

This combination is in Group A.
Turn to page 375.
Italicized words further
explained in the glossary.

Venus in Libra and Mars in Virgo

ROMANCE

is *erratic*. Opposite elements are working: prodigal air and dense earth. This one has style—but the beat is uncertain. This one is cavalier, but something is reluctant. This one operates on a high, remote plane. This one is clinical, cautious, conservative, cold, unresponsive—has difficulty with romance, doesn't trust romance. This one can't handle the unknown.

LOVE

is *chaotic*. Affections are stuttering, emotions are subdued. There is a brilliance, a charm, but there are inner crosscurrents. This one reaches for the quintessential—but is too pragmatic, too analytical. This one has difficulty with love, can't put it all up, doesn't know how to give. There is no enthusiasm, no rhythm, no expanse. There is something defensive.

PASSION

is *tumultuous*. Pent-up energies are released. This one serves to indulge, to entertain, to ingratiate. This one relates to touch, knows nerve centers. Nothing is undone, nothing withheld. It's all *hyper*, all confused. Physical exchange is *pursuit of fantasy*.

GUIDELINES

You can get hurt. This combination is unstable. Play this one *short term*.

This combination is in Group C.
Turn to page 379.
Italicized words further
explained in the glossary.

Venus in Libra
and
Mars in Libra

ROMANCE

starts quickly. Exact same elements are working. This
one is all perfumed air, reaching for the quintessential.
The style is refined. This one is balanced, has dignity,
direction. This one is honorable, discriminating,
intelligent. There is grace, charm, rhythm. Imagination adds to the speed, aspiration adds to the lift, the
thing soars—romance takes wing. This one operates in
the heavens.

LOVE

is *good times.* Affections are rich, emotions are deep.
Idealism propels, purpose takes this one up. This one
lives to love, loves to love, brings brilliance to love.
The beat is unstoppable: there is devotion, enchant-
ment, total commitment. This one is designed for love,
can orchestrate, has a mystical knack. This one shapes
dreams into reality.

PASSION

is *sacred duty*. This one is mental, serves to support, to inspire, to nurture. This one is intuitive, *uncanny*, knows nerve centers. Something is transcendent. Nothing is denied—it's all *ultra*. There is continuity. Physical exchange is *culmination of love*.

GUIDELINES

You can't get hurt. This combination is stable (one love at a time). Play this one *long term*.

This combination is in Group A.
Turn to page 375.
Italicized words further
explained in the glossary.

Venus in Libra
and
Mars in Scorpio

ROMANCE

is *erratic*. Opposite elements are working: prodigal air and uncontrolled water. This one is magnetic, has power—but inner systems are disorganized. This one is extreme, driven...hyper-intense, hyper-forceful, hyper-determined. This one plays a game—romance is just a prelude. This one is deep, mystical, unstoppable. Something calls this one. The fury of a wild wind whips the tides into a churning frenzy.

LOVE

is *chaotic*. Affections are lavish, emotions are fierce. Appetites propel, fearlessness adds to the speed, lack of restraint takes this one too far out. This one is untiring, unrelenting, diabolical. This one pursues love, uses love. This one won't be denied. This one needs to feed. The tides pound against the dike.

PASSION

is *tumultuous*. Obsessive pent-up energies are released. This one serves to indulge, to consume, to nurture. The juices flow. This one relates to touch, knows nerve centers, is *uncanny*. Nothing is undone, nothing withheld. It's all *hyper*, all confused. Physical exchange is *pursuit of fantasy*.

GUIDELINES

You can get hurt. This combination is unstable. Play this one *short term*.

This combination is in Group C.
Turn to page 379.
Italicized words further
explained in the glossary.

Venus in Libra
and
Mars in Sagittarius

ROMANCE

starts quickly. Combining elements are working: perfumed air and low-keyed fire. The style is easy, controlled. There is contained idealism, character, humor, rhythm. There is nothing frivolous, nothing disruptive. This one knows how to build—can cope, can manage, can steer. This one is reliable. Romance grows. Something sparkles, the air is intoxicating, the sun comes up. There is early morning magic.

LOVE

is *good times.* Affections are friendly, emotions are deep. This one is no fool. There is quiet power. This one is resourceful, sophisticated, confident...keeps love together, relates to commitment, understands love, delivers essentials. The thing flows evenly. This one has the knack—the efficient entrepreneur. This one faces the future coolly, shaping destiny.

PASSION

is *sacred duty*. This one is mental, serves to support, to assure, to inspire. This one responds to need—nothing is denied. It's all well-intentioned, all with grace. There is continuity. Physical exchange is *expression of faith*.

GUIDELINES

You can't get hurt. This combination is stable (one love at a time). Play this one *long term*.

This combination is in Group B.
Turn to page 377.
Italicized words further
explained in the glossary.

Venus in Libra
and
Mars in Capricorn

ROMANCE
is *erratic*. Opposite elements are working: prodigal air
and dense earth. Inner systems are disorganized. This
one is unpredictable, uncontrolled—without direction, without intuition. This one can't see, can't steer,
can't cope. This one is insecure, narrow-minded,
petty. There are jealousies. Romance can't build,
romance can't grow. This one can't give, is an
amateur. This one rides an ostrich.

LOVE
is *chaotic*. Affections are without conviction, emotions
are stunted. There is no inspiration, no confidence.
This one is defensive, cautious, pessimistic, clumsy.
There are stuttering involvements, scattered commitments...no rhythm. Love stumbles, can't build. This
one is too hard to reach. This one spins. A dark cloud
overhangs.

PASSION

is *tumultuous*. Pent-up energies are released. This one serves to indulge, to consume, to ingratiate. There is something carnal. This one knows nerve centers. Nothing is undone, nothing withheld. It's all *hyper*, all confused. Physical exchange is *pursuit of fantasy*.

GUIDELINES

You can get hurt. This combination is unstable. Play this one *short term*.

This combination is in Group C.
Turn to page 379.
Italicized words further
explained in the glossary.

Venus in Libra
and
Mars in Aquarius

ROMANCE

starts quickly. Similar elements are working. This one is perfumed vibrant air—the spirit takes wing. This one reaches up, aspires, is good-natured, with a liberal attitude. This one is honorable, has humor, control, rhythm, direction, confidence. There is nothing stupid, nothing maudlin. This one brings vitality to romance. There is sparkle—a divine spark.

LOVE

is *good times.* Affections are free-flowing, emotions are deep. These are warm prevailing winds. This one relates to duty, is noble. There is intuition, sympathy, understanding, tolerance. This one can manage, can cope, is resourceful. There is something mature. Love builds, love conquers all. There is excellence. This one is the dedicated tireless genie.

PASSION

is *tremendous*. This one is mental, serves to support, to assure, to inspire. This one is giving, knows nerve centers. Nothing is denied. It's all with grace; there is continuity. Physical exchange is *expression of faith*.

GUIDELINES

You can't get hurt. This combination is stable (one love at a time). Play this one *long term*.

This combination is in Group B.
Turn to page 377.
Italicized words further
explained in the glossary.

Venus in Libra
and
Mars in Pisces

ROMANCE

is *erratic*. Opposite elements are working: uncontainable air and uncontainable water. This one can't resist adventure...new involvements. This one is impressionistic, pliable, quixotic. The imagination is uncontrolled—there are wild flights. There is something unknowing, a madness. Impulse is ruinous. This one spins. There are entanglements. Romance can't build, is without depth. This one can't concentrate.

LOVE

is *chaotic*. Affections are easily induced, emotions are extravagant. This one is too extreme, can't handle love, gives too much too soon. There is a paralysis of will. This one can't cope, can't anticipate...is too receptive, too open...self-deceptive. There are shocks, disappointments. The beat is wild—love is elusive. There is something misbegotten. This one can't steer, can't find love. Confidence breaks down, aspirations fade, there is loss of momentum. This one is unlucky; a dark cloud hangs over.

PASSION

is *tumultuous*. Pent-up energies are released. This one serves to indulge, to entertain, to lavish. This one is intuitive, *uncanny*—knows nerve centers, relates to touch. It's all *hyper*. There is confusion. Physical exchange is *pursuit of fulfillment*.

GUIDELINES

You can get hurt. This combination is unstable. Play this one *short term*.

This combination is in Group C.
Turn to page 379.
Italicized words further
explained in the glossary.

Venus in Scorpio and Mars in Aries

ROMANCE

is *erratic*. Opposite elements are working: uncontrolled water and scorching fire. There is inner turmoil, wild momentum. This one is overbearing, impatient, conceited, flamboyant, too aggressive, reckless. There is no rhythm, no grace, no balance, no direction. There are explosions, confrontations, entanglements. Romance is in unknowing hands; romance can't build. This one is the unsophisticated Viking.

LOVE

is *chaotic*. Affections are fierce, emotions are quick to erupt. There is violence. This one is domineering, tyrannical, possessive, jealous. There are storms—the temper is inflammable, without humor, without tact. There are obsessions, extremes. Love can't build; love can't survive. The heat is blistering: steam fills the lungs.

PASSION

is *tumultuous*. Pent-up energies are released. This one serves to indulge, to lavish, to conquer. This one doesn't relate to touch...the method is harsh...no intuition. Nothing is undone, but it's all too intense, all *hyper*. Physical exchange is *pursuit of fantasy*.

GUIDELINES

You can get hurt. This combination is unstable. Play this one *short term*.

This combination is in Group C.
Turn to page 379.
Italicized words further
explained in the glossary.

Venus in Scorpio and Mars in Taurus

ROMANCE

starts slowly. Combining elements are working: surging water and pulsating earth. This one is magnetic, with charm, grace, veiled power, control, direction. There is nothing frivolous. This one can cope, can manage. The beat is irresistible. There is an emergence—romance builds. There are buddings. Romance is in strong hands: it's all lush, all promising. Something is magical.

LOVE

grows. Affections are rich, emotions are deep. This one relates to love, knows love, feeds love. This one is constant, fearless, intelligent—takes care of love, is parental. Love is sacred toil. There is compassion, depth, purpose. Love builds. There is a greening, a blooming. It's all intoxicating.

PASSION

is *tremendous*. This one communicates by touch, serves
to replenish, to comfort, to nurture. This one knows
nerve centers, is intuitive, *uncanny*. Nothing is denied.
It's all well-intentioned. Something is *ultra*. There is
continuity. Physical exchange is *culmination of love*.

GUIDELINES

You can't get hurt. This combination is stable (one love at
a time). Play this one *long term*.

This combination is in Group A.
Turn to page 375.
Italicized words further
explained in the glossary.

Venus in Scorpio
and
Mars in Gemini

ROMANCE
is *erratic*. Opposite elements are working: uncontrolled water and restless air. There is something clever, something captivating, but inner systems are disorganized. This one is too easily involved, no direction. Impulse propels, nervous energy adds to the speed, lack of character takes this one too far out. Romance is just a game. The compass spins, there are involvements, entanglements. Romance can't build. This one deals in passing fancies.

LOVE
is *chaotic*. Affections are quick-developing, emotions are quick-passing. This one doesn't relate to love, can't build love. This one is superficial. Commitments are scattered. There is noise without meaning... aspirations are thin... love is just a word. This one suddenly disappears. Whimsical winds drive grey clouds in front of the sun.

PASSION

is *tumultuous*. Pent-up energies are released. This one serves to indulge, to entertain, to ingratiate. This one is mental—doesn't relate to touch: sensations are colorless. It's all confused. This one is *hyper*. There is no continuity. Physical exchange is *escape from reality*.

GUIDELINES

You can get hurt. This combination is unstable. Play this one *short term*.

This combination is in Group D.
Turn to page 381.
Italicized words further
explained in the glossary

Venus in Scorpio
and
Mars in Cancer

ROMANCE

starts slowly. Similar elements are working. This one is surging pulsating water, deep, profound, subtle. There is nothing stupid, nothing flamboyant. This one is balanced—has direction, honor, grace, magnetism. This one is ultra-receptive. The heart is good. Romance builds; romance is magical. There are clear reflections out of a quiet hidden pool.

LOVE

grows. Affections are lavish, emotions are devotional. This one knows love, operates best when in love. This one is parental—the flow is warm. This one is protective, intuitive. This one can cope, keeps it all together. There is conviction, timing. This one knows what to do, how to go. Love is in good hands. There is purpose. This one has quality. Something emerges. This one is mystical, luminescent. All things dance to the pull of the moon.

PASSION

is *tremendous*. This one communicates by touch, serves to replenish, to comfort, to nurture. There is a gushing. This one knows nerve centers, is *uncanny*. Nothing is denied. This one is sensual, this one is *ultra*. There is continuity. Physical exchange is *culmination of love*.

GUIDELINES

You can't get hurt. This combination is stable (one love at a time). Play this one *long term*.

This combination is in Group A.
Turn to page 375.
Italicized words further
explained in the glossary.

Venus in Scorpio
and
Mars in Leo

ROMANCE

is *erratic*. Opposite elements are working: surging water and uncontrolled fire. There is inner conflict—no balance, no direction. This one is too bold, brash, impetuous, aggressive, forceful, militant, unbridled, inflammable. There are blowups, disruptions, entanglements. The beat is wild; romance can't build. This one rides a dragon.

LOVE

is *chaotic*. Affections are quick-erupting, emotions are unrestricted. This one is extravagant—the unknowing entrepreneur. There is no tact, no intuition. This one can't see, can't steer, charges headlong into catastrophes. There is conceit, arrogance. There are shocks. Love can't build, can't grow. This one dives from cliffs but misjudges the depth of the water.

PASSION

is *tumultuous*. Pent-up energies are released. This one
serves to indulge, to lavish, to ingratiate. There is
awesome surge, there are acrobatics. Nothing is
undone, nothing withheld. It's all confused, all *hyper*.
Physical exchange is *escape from reality*.

GUIDELINES

You can get hurt. This combination is unstable. Play this
one *short term*.

This combination is in Group D.
Turn to page 381.
Italicized words further
explained in the glossary.

Venus in Scorpio
and
Mars in Virgo

ROMANCE
starts slowly. Combining elements are working: surging water and soft earth. There is quiet efficiency: organization, direction, control, rhythm, timing. There is nothing disruptive, nothing theatrical. This one has character. This one is capable, cool, calm, soothing. There is intuition. The beat is steady— romance is in knowing hands, romance builds. There is something mature: an ability to keep the thing going. This one takes care of business, has the knack.

LOVE
grows. Affections are balanced, emotions are regulated. This one understands commitment, rises to commitment. This one is assuring, supportive, contributive, family, loyal, intelligent. This one has depth, quality. Love takes hold, love builds. The dike opens permissively, the water flows, the earth drinks. There is a greening, life is ongoing, love endures. It's all high-level.

PASSION

is *tremendous*. This one communicates by touch, serves to replenish, to comfort, to inspire. This one knows nerve centers, is therapeutic, *uncanny*. Nothing is denied, it's all honest, all with grace. There is continuity. Physical exchange is *expression of faith*.

GUIDELINES

You can't get hurt. This combination is stable (one love at a time). Play this one *long term*.

This combination is in Group B.
Turn to page 377.
Italicized words further
explained in the glossary.

Venus in Scorpio and Mars in Libra

.

ROMANCE

is *erratic*. Opposite elements are working: uncontrolled water and prodigal air. This one has style, charm. This one can be fascinating, but inner systems are disorganized. This one is extreme, goes in all directions—with no restraint, no discretion. Impulse is ruinous. There are entanglements. The beat is wild; romance can't build. This one lives in an ever-changing dream.

LOVE

is *chaotic*. Affections are lavish, emotions are uncontrollable. This one lives to love, but can't handle love—gives too much too soon, expects too much too soon. There is no rhythm, no timing. This one can't play the game, doesn't anticipate. There are mad flights, whimsical crusades. This one can't deal with reality. This one is fraudulent evangelist.

PASSION

is *tumultuous*. Deep pent-up energies are released. This one serves to indulge, to entertain, to nurture. This one is intuitive, knows nerve centers. Nothing is undone, nothing withheld. This one may be carnal, is *hyper*, confused. Physical exchange is *pursuit of fantasy*.

GUIDELINES

You can get hurt. This combination is unstable. Play this one *short term*.

This combination is in Group C.
Turn to page 379.
Italicized words further
explained in the glossary.

Venus in Scorpio
and
Mars in Scorpio

ROMANCE

starts slowly. Exact same elements are working. This one is all surging water—magnetic, powerful, controlled. There is charm, grace, intelligence. This one is intuitive, perceptive, reliable, courageous, honorable. There is nothing impulsive, nothing frivolous. This one is determined. The beat is strong; romance builds, romance has depth. There is an irresistible pull. This one is streams flowing into rivers, rivers flowing into oceans.

LOVE

grows. Affections are rich, emotions are deep. This one lives to love, needs to love, feeds on love—knows love, takes care of love. This one is constant, protective, supportive, untiring, unswerving. There is total commitment, arch intensity. It all comes together. This one shapes destiny.

PASSION

is *tremendous*. This one communicates by touch, serves to replenish, to comfort, to nurture. There is a voluptuousness. This one knows nerve centers, is *uncanny*. Nothing is denied; it's all *ultra*. There is continuity. Physical exchange is *culmination of love*.

GUIDELINES

You can't get hurt. This combination is stable (one love at a time). Play this one *long term*.

This combination is in Group A.
Turn to page 375.
Italicized words further
explained in the glossary.

Venus in Scorpio and Mars in Sagittarius

ROMANCE

is *erratic*. Opposite elements are working: uncontrolled water and unrestricted fire. This one is wild, has no balance, no direction, no restraint. Inner systems are disorganized. Impulse propels, recklessness adds to the speed, lack of morality takes this one too far out. There are involvements, entanglements. Romance is in irresponsible hands, romance can't sustain. This one flies planes into mountains.

LOVE

is *chaotic*. Affections are shallow, emotions are theatrical. This one doesn't relate to love, has no need for love, doesn't want love. Relationships are quick-passing—just flashes of interest, quick-fading. There is nothing constant, nothing deep. Love can't build. This one plays games: it's all façade, all shadows. There is nothing of value.

PASSION

is *tumultuous*. Pent-up energies are released. This one serves to indulge, to entertain, to ingratiate. Anything goes when the whistle blows. This one is carnal. Nothing is undone, nothing withheld. It's all *hyper*. There is no continuity. Physical exchange is *escape from reality*.

GUIDELINES

You can get hurt. This combination is unstable. Play this one *short term*.

This combination is in Group D.
Turn to page 381.
Italicized words further
explained in the glossary.

Venus in Scorpio and Mars in Capricorn

ROMANCE

starts slowly. Combining elements are working: surging water and receptive earth. This one has strength, depth, operates efficiently. There are no theatrics—there is an easy rhythm, humor, finesse. This one is the capable entrepreneur. This one can orchestrate. The beat is strong; romance builds. There is wine. There is something auspicious.

LOVE

grows. Affections are warm, emotions are powerful. This one knows love, can handle love . . . is supportive, contributive. There is compassion, understanding. This one can be fiercely protective, intuitively gentle, reliable. Love stays on course. This one is the intelligent captain of an ocean liner.

PASSION

is *tremendous*. This one communicates by touch, serves to replenish, to comfort, to nurture. This one knows nerve centers, is *uncanny*. Nothing is denied. There is a steady release of unstoppable energy, all high-level. There is continuity. Physical exchange is *rendezvous with destiny*.

GUIDELINES

You can't get hurt. This combination is stable (one love at a time). Play this one *long term*.

This combination is in Group B.
Turn to page 377.
Italicized words further
explained in the glossary.

Venus in Scorpio and Mars in Aquarius

ROMANCE

is *erratic*. Opposite elements are working: uncontrolled water and uncontrollable air. Inner systems are disorganized. This one is too temptable, too impressionable, too easily persuaded. Impulse propels, good will adds to the speed, lack of intuition takes this one down. There are frustrations, disappointments, blind alleys. This one is tossed—amateur, bewildered. Romance can't build. There is nothing auspicious. There are shocks. A limping gazelle catches the eye of a lioness.

LOVE

is *chaotic*. Affections are frivolous, emotions are limited. There is no confidence. This one can't sift, can't sort, can't steer. There are instant commitments, entanglements. This one stabs at love—is too sporting, reckless, masochistic. This one spins. The beat is wild; love has no chance. There is no luck. This one loses at Russian Roulette.

PASSION

is *tumultuous*. Pent-up energies are released. This one serves to soothe, to entertain, to ingratiate. Anything goes when the whistle blows. There are acrobatics; nothing is undone. There is something bizarre—it's all without meaning, all *hyper*. Physical exchange is *escape from reality*.

GUIDELINES

You can get hurt. This combination is unstable. Play this one *short term*.

This combination is in Group D.
Turn to page 381.
Italicized words further
explained in the glossary.

Venus in Scorpio
and
Mars in Pisces

ROMANCE

starts slowly. Similar elements are working. This one is surging sweet water. This one is the quiet, efficient manager: perceptive, intelligent, sophisticated—supportive, contributive, sympathetic. This one has humor, taste, rhythm. This one keeps good things going—knows romance, builds romance. There is a velvet mist . . . wine . . . music. There is magical emergence.

LOVE

grows. Affections are lush, emotions are deep. This one flows with love, lives to love, loves to love. The style is voluptuous, the giving is endless, the yielding is graceful. There is tact, discretion, intuition. This one can cope, can anticipate, can handle pressure. This one is smooth, reassuring, devoted—keeps love together, can orchestrate. The water in the lagoon is clear, the tide is gentle, beautiful fish swim easily. There is harmony.

PASSION

is *tremendous*. This one communicates by touch, serves to replenish, to comfort, to nurture. The juices flow. This one knows nerve centers, is *uncanny*, sends shivers. Nothing is denied. It's all high-level, all well-intentioned. There is continuity. Physical exchange is *rendezvous with destiny*.

GUIDELINES

You can't get hurt. This combination is stable (one love at a time). Play this one *long term*.

This combination is in Group B.
Turn to page 377.
Italicized words further
explained in the glossary.

Venus in Sagittarius and Mars in Aries

ROMANCE

starts quickly. Similar elements are working. This one is non-scorching brilliant fire. The style is exciting. This one is big, controlled . . . has courage, humor, grace, confidence. Idealism propels, pursuit of adventure adds to the speed, intelligence gives direction. This one takes charge, leads the charge, knows how to keep romance going. It's all without ego, all positive. Romance builds—something sparkles, something pulses with promise.

LOVE

is *good times.* Affections are free-flowing, emotions are deep. This one relates to love, lives to love, can handle love. This one has the knack, can see, can steer, can cope, can manage. This one may be overbearing, may be too dominant—but it's all well-intentioned, all pure enthusiasm. This one is supportive, protective, constant, parental. Love is in strong hands. There is a dawning, an unstoppable rising. The sun comes over the horizon.

PASSION

is *sacred duty*. This one is mental—serves to assure, to inspire, to nurture. Energy is released directly. This one responds to need; nothing is denied. It's all high-level. There is continuity. Physical exchange is *rendezvous with destiny*.

GUIDELINES

You can't get hurt. This combination is stable (one love at a time). Play this one *long term*.

This combination is in Group B.
Turn to page 377.
Italicized words further
explained in the glossary.

Venus in Sagittarius
and
Mars in Taurus

ROMANCE

is *erratic*. Opposite elements are working: unrestricted
fire and dense earth. Inner systems are disorganized.
This one is too turned inward, too self-serving, too
self-indulgent. This one can't give—is insecure,
unimaginative, hesitating. There is no intuition, no
confidence. Romance can't build. This one can't see,
can't steer. There is no rhythm. This one goes in
circles. There are entanglements, madness.

LOVE

is *chaotic*. Affections are superficial, emotions are
groping. Love is just a word, an empty game. This one
is too remote to reach, too immovable to inspire—love
can't grow. The sun shines without warmth, the earth
is unreceptive, seedlings have trouble taking root. This
one doesn't trust love, doesn't know how to handle
love. It's all frustrating, anti-climactic. This one is dry.

PASSION

is *tumultuous*. Pent-up energies are released. This one serves to indulge, to entertain, to ingratiate. This one relates to touch. There is erotic intuition. Nothing is undone, nothing withheld, but it's all confused, all *hyper*. Physical exchange is *pursuit of fantasy*.

GUIDELINES

You can get hurt. This combination is unstable. Play this one *short term*.

This combination is in Group C.
Turn to page 379.
Italicized words further
explained in the glossary.

Venus in Sagittarius and Mars in Gemini

ROMANCE

starts quickly. Combining elements are working: low-keyed fire and controlled air. This one has tempo, timing, intelligence, grace, humor, sophistication. This one is perceptive, can see, can anticipate—handles romance expertly. This one is professional, reliable, resourceful; this one can steer. Romance builds. This one has nerve, bringing the spaceship back to earth safely.

LOVE

is *good times.* Affections are regulated, emotions are balanced. This one is mature. Inner systems work smoothly. This one cuts through dilemmas, can handle pressure. The beat is strong. There is nothing frivolous, nothing flamboyant. This one knows how to take care of love, knows how to keep love together, can manage. Love is in capable hands—the constant buddy, the abiding musketeer. Love sustains. There is cheerful comradery.

LOVE

is *sacred duty*. This one is mental: serves to comfort, to assure, to inspire. This one responds to need. Energy is released directly. Nothing is denied. It's all well-intentioned; there is continuity. Physical exchange is *expression of faith*.

GUIDELINES

You can't get hurt. This combination is stable (one love at a time). Play this one *long term*.

This combination is in Group B.
Turn to page 377.
Italicized words further
explained in the glossary.

Venus in Sagittarius and Mars in Cancer

ROMANCE

is *erratic*. Opposite elements are working: unrestricted fire and dense water. Inner systems are disorganized. This one can't operate evenly—there is no rhythm. This one is fickle, changeable, unpredictable ... can't handle social situations ... is too turned inward, too self-serving, too self-indulgent. This one can't give, can't receive, can't see, can't anticipate. There is no timing. Romance can't build. There is something limited, something muddled, something uncertain. There are shocks, collisions, entanglements. This one can't steer.

LOVE

is *chaotic*. Affections are theatrical, emotions are shallow. This one plays a game, uses love—an amateur entrepreneur. There is something petty. This one commits for profit, must receive more than is given, is too demanding, too stifling. There is nothing aspirational or towering, no expanse, no grace. Love is exhausting. This one is afraid of love. There are inner storms.

PASSION

is *tumultuous*. Deep pent-up energies are released. This one serves to indulge, to ingratiate, to nurture. This one relates to touch, knows nerve centers. The juices flow. There is erotic intuition. Nothing is undone, nothing withheld—but it's all confused, all *hyper*. Physical exchange is *pursuit of fantasy*.

GUIDELINES

You can get hurt. This combination is unstable. Play this one *short term*.

This combination is in Group C.
Turn to page 379.
Italicized words further
explained in the glossary.

Venus in Sagittarius and Mars in Leo

ROMANCE

starts quickly. Similar elements are working. This one is low-keyed nurturing fire. Inner systems are smooth-running. This one has the knack—the style is easy, strong; there is balance, direction. This one is honorable, sporting, sophisticated. This one has it all: intelligence, gentility, understanding, rhythm, humor. It's all high-level. Romance builds, grows. There is shining purpose. The sun comes up.

LOVE

is *good times*. Affections are warm, emotions are deep. This one is equal to love, can steer, can cope—can manage love, feed love, cradle love. There is maturity, reliability, efficiency. This one gets the job done. Love endures, survives, shines. Love rises. There is a rugged nobility.

PASSION

is *sacred duty*. This one is mental—serves to comfort, to assure, to inspire. This one responds to need. There is straight-out release of positive energy; nothing is denied. It's all with grace, all well-intentioned. There is continuity. Physical exchange is *expression of faith*.

GUIDELINES

You can't get hurt. This combination is stable (one love at a time). Play this one *long term*.

This combination is in Group B.
Turn to page 377.
Italicized words further
explained in the glossary.

Venus in Sagittarius
and
Mars in Virgo

ROMANCE

is *erratic*. Opposite elements are working: unrestricted
fire and barren earth. Inner systems are disorganized—
scattered. There are no convictions, no intuition, no
imagination. This one is too detached, too remote, too
cold, too objective, too clinical. This one is agnostic.
There is no oxygen. Romance can't build. This one is
the barren surface of the moon.

LOVE

is *chaotic*. Affections are thin, emotions are transient.
This one is incapable of giving. There is no ore, no
sentiment, no sympathy, no compassion. This one is
bloodless. Love is just a word—love is locked out. This
one doesn't care, takes what comes, plays it minute to
minute. There is nothing towering, nothing idealistic.
The confidence is theatrical, the poise is momentary.
It's all without rhythm—pale, by rote. There is noise
without meaning.

PASSION

is *tumultuous*. Pent-up energies are released. This one serves to indulge, to entertain, to ingratiate. Anything goes when the whistle blows. This one relates to touch; there is erotic intuition. Nothing is undone, nothing withheld, but it's all confused, all *hyper*. There is no continuity. Physical exchange is *escape from reality*.

GUIDELINES

You can get hurt. This combination is unstable. Play this one *short term*.

This combination is in Group D.
Turn to page 381.
Italicized words further
explained in the glossary.

Venus in Sagittarius and Mars in Libra

ROMANCE

starts quickly. Combining elements are working: low-keyed fire and perfumed air. There is an easy style, humor, grace, charm. This one is refined, balanced, has tact and timing. This one is together, can steer, has confidence. The beat is steady. This one has imagination—reaches out for romance, reaches up for romance. There is sparkling idealism. Romance takes wing. There is golden purpose. This one knows the road to Camelot.

LOVE

is *good times*. Affections are dignified, emotions are deep. This one lives for love, is motivated by love, is designed for love. There is nothing rash, nothing frivolous. This one is intuitive, tender, reliable, honest. This one knows how to give, how to support, how to build, how to keep it going. This one can manage, can cope. There is cool, clear judgment. This one has rhythm, taste, sophistication. Love is in good hands. There is beauty, music, shining aspiration. It's all high-level. There is magic in the air.

PASSION

is *tremendous*. This one is mental—serves to comfort, to inspire, to nurture. There is a soaring. This one responds to need, knows nerve centers. Nothing is denied. It's all well-intentioned. There is continuity. Physical exchange is *rendezvous with destiny*.

GUIDELINES

You can't get hurt. This combination is stable (one love at a time). Play this one *long term*.

This combination is in Group B.
Turn to page 377.
Italicized words further
explained in the glossary.

Venus in Sagittarius and Mars in Scorpio

ROMANCE

is *erratic*. Opposite elements are working: unrestricted fire and uncontrolled water. Inner systems are disorganized, without direction, without balance, without control. There is no rhythm, no grace—no sensitivity, no sympathy. This one is dishonest, callous, indiscriminate. Romance is just empty ritual. This one looks beyond romance. There are schemes, intrigue. Powers of darkness drive this one—the diabolical entrepreneur. There is something ominous. There are whirlpools.

LOVE

is *chaotic*. Affections are calculated, emotions are powerful. This one is the artful tempter, using love. This one is cunning. There is black magic. The beat is irresistible, but there is nothing inspirational, nothing lyrical. Something self-gratifying motivates, something self-serving compels. Love is just a meaningless game, a device, a web.

PASSION

is *tumultuous*. Deep pent-up energies are released. This one serves to indulge, to lavish, to ingratiate. Anything goes when the whistle blows. The juices flow; there is erotic intuition. This one knows nerve centers, is *uncanny*. There is steam heat. It's all madness, all *hyper*. There is no continuity. Physical exchange is *escape from reality*.

GUIDELINES

You can get hurt. This combination is unstable. Play this one *short term*.

This combination is in Group D.
Turn to page 381.
Italicized words further
explained in the glossary.

Venus in Sagittarius and Mars in Sagittarius

ROMANCE

starts quickly. Exact same elements are working: all low-keyed fire. This one is cool, efficient, modulated. There is direction, control, balance. Inner systems are finely tuned. There is tact, discretion, sophistication. This one can orchestrate, can compensate, can maneuver, can steer. This one is reliable, adult, worldly. Romance is in superb hands. Romance builds—there is cool brilliance. All arrows find the center of the target.

LOVE

is *good times*. Affections are mature, emotions are constant. There are no pipe dreams, no trips to the moon, nothing frivolous. This one gets the job done, can anticipate—knows human deficiencies, human frailties. This one can cope, can handle pressure. There is gut intelligence, gut strength. This one is the tough, straight-shooting, idealistic sheriff, keeping love together. There is peace in the valley.

PASSION

is *sacred duty*. This one is mental—serves to comfort, to assure, to inspire. This one responds to need, is therapeutic. Nothing is denied. It's all well-intentioned; there is continuity. Physical exchange is *expression of faith*.

GUIDELINES

You can't get hurt. This combination is stable (one love at a time). Play this one *long term*.

This combination is in Group B.
Turn to page 377.
Italicized words further
explained in the glossary.

Venus in Sagittarius
and
Mars in Capricorn

ROMANCE

is *erratic*. Opposite elements are working: restricted fire
and dense earth. There is inner turmoil. This one is
unpredictable . . . without imagination, without color,
without gaiety . . . dry, unknowing. There is uncon-
tained impulse, raw force. The beat is disjointed. This
one gropes for romance. There is something gloomy,
reckless, tossed—romance can't build. This one is
without luck. The glitter fades quickly.

LOVE

is *chaotic*. Affections are superficial, emotions are cold.
This one is hesitant, muddled, defensive. There is no
sweet flow, no happiness. The scope is limited. There is
no charm, no grace. This one must receive more than is
given, doesn't know how to give. This one is weak,
gross, blundering—can't manage, can't steer. Love
can't grow: it is without conviction. There are
entanglements, catastrophes. There is no direction, no
divine spark.

PASSION

is *tumultuous*. Pent-up energies are released. This one serves to indulge, to lavish, to ingratiate. Anything goes when the whistle blows. This one knows nerve centers, is *uncanny*. Nothing is undone, nothing withheld—it's all confused, all *hyper*. There is no continuity. Physical exchange is *escape from reality*.

GUIDELINES

You can get hurt. This combination is unstable. Play this one *short term*.

This combination is in Group D.
Turn to page 381.
Italicized words further
explained in the glossary.

Venus in Sagittarius and Mars in Aquarius

ROMANCE

starts quickly. Combining elements are working: low-keyed fire and vibrant air. Inner systems are sturdily constructed. This one operates without ceremony, without theatrics. This one is sincere, sociable, well-intentioned. This one has sympathy, insight, humor. This one reaches out, reaches up—there are aspirations. There is gentility, grace, honor, courage. Romance builds—it is in good hands. The city bird comes through winter undaunted.

LOVE

is *good times.* Affections are smooth-flowing, emotions are noble. This one believes in love, is inspired by love, rises to love. This one gives more than is received—is warm, supportive, protective, compassionate, positive, liberal, mature. This one can steer, can cope. There is rhythm, enthusiasm, optimism. The beat is steady, the heart is good. Love has substance, love grows. There is the resourcefulness to sustain. This one is the capable pioneer crossing the country in a covered wagon.

PASSION

is *sacred duty*. This one is mental—serves to comfort, to assure, to inspire. This one responds to need, is therapeutic. Nothing is denied. It's all high-level. There is continuity. Physical exchange is *expression of faith*.

GUIDELINES

You can't get hurt. This combination is stable (one love at a time). Play this one *long term*.

This combination is in Group B.
Turn to page 377.
Italicized words further
explained in the glossary.

Venus in Sagittarius and Mars in Pisces

ROMANCE

is *erratic*. Opposite elements are working: unrestricted fire and churning water. This one is unsynchronized. There are inner storms—this one is tossed. There is misfortune, no intuition, no rhythm, no confidence. This one is vulnerable...too open, too receptive...too easily swayed, impressed, duped. There are infatuations, wild flights. Impulse is ruinous, judgment is amateur. Romance can't build—it has no chance. This one is a herring in a net.

LOVE

is *chaotic*. Affections are fleeting, emotions are hesitant. This one is unknowing. There is indecision, timidity. This one can't see, can't cope. Love is one gamble after another. This one clutches at love, gropes for love— but it is elusive. There is no poise, no balance, no conviction. This one goes in all directions at once. This one is a small voice in the wilderness.

PASSION

is *tumultuous*. Pent-up energies are released. This one serves to indulge, to lavish, to ingratiate. Anything goes when the whistle blows. This one knows nerve centers, is *uncanny*. Nothing is undone, but it's all confused, all *hyper*—there is no continuity. Physical exchange is *escape from reality*.

GUIDELINES

You can get hurt. This combination is unstable. Play this one *short term*.

This combination is in Group D.
Turn to page 381.
Italicized words further
explained in the glossary.

Venus in Capricorn
and
Mars in Aries

ROMANCE

is *erratic*. Opposite elements are working: dense earth and scorching fire. There is inner upheaval—no balance, no consistency, no direction. This one is volatile, eruptive, reckless. Impulse is ruinous. This one is domineering, headstrong, without perception, without sensitivity. There is madness. The style is harsh. Romance can't build; romance has no chance. Lions are attacking the horses.

LOVE

is *chaotic*. Affections are rash, emotions are tempestuous. There are tantrums, tempers, belligerence, jealousy, possessiveness. There are extremes, nothing lyrical. The violence is too disruptive. There is no intuition, no timing, no patience. Love has no chance—can't build, can't grow. The desert sun is too hot, the desert night too cold.

PASSION

is *tumultuous*. Obsessive pent-up energies are released. This one serves to conquer, to lavish, to nurture. There is awesome surge—the action is furious. Nothing is undone, nothing withheld. It's all *hyper*, all confused. Physical exchange is *pursuit of fantasy*.

GUIDELINES

You can get hurt. This combination is unstable. Play this one *short term*.

This combination is in Group C.
Turn to page 379.
Italicized words further
explained in the glossary.

Venus in Capricorn and Mars in Taurus

ROMANCE

starts slowly. Similar elements are working. This one is receptive pulsating earth, reliable, determined, practical. There is intuition, tact, discretion. This one can orchestrate, can cope, can anticipate. There is power, conviction, honesty. This one has it all—grace, humor, charm, depth, courage. The beat is firm. Romance builds. There is wine ... a fragrance ... soft music. The atmosphere is lush.

LOVE

grows. Affections are warm, emotions are deep. There is nothing frivolous, nothing maudlin. This one is no fool, is perceptive, discriminating. This one can steer—knows love, relates to love, needs to love, feeds on love, comes alive with love, reaches fulfillment through love. There is total commitment: a blooming, a flowering. The elements dance, the beat is strong. Love emerges a towering thing. There is grandeur.

PASSION

is *tremendous*. This one communicates by touch, serves to replenish, to comfort, to nurture. The pores open, the juices flow. Nothing is denied. It's all high-level, all *ultra*. There is continuity. Physical exchange is *culmination of love.*

GUIDELINES

You can't get hurt. This combination is stable (one love at a time). Play this one *long term*.

This combination is in Group A.
Turn to page 375.
Italicized words further
explained in the glossary.

Venus in Capricorn
and
Mars in Gemini

ROMANCE

is *erratic*. Opposite elements are working: dense earth and uncontainable air. Inner systems are disorganized—impatience is ruinous. This one can't concentrate, can't focus. There is no balance, no direction. This one is cold, anti-social, nervous. There are wild flights, distractions, entanglements. There is confusion, deceit, something rakish. Romance spins, can't build, fades quickly. The glitter is thin.

LOVE

is *chaotic*. Affections are transitory, emotions are theatrical. This one doesn't relate to love—is elusive, footloose, superficial. This one flirts with love, plays games with love. It's all at arm's length: there are just flashes of interest, nothing deep, nothing abiding. This one is minor, without color. Love can't grow, goes nowhere. This one is dry, remote, unfeeling. There is just the rustle of the wind.

PASSION

is *tumultuous*. Pent-up energies are released. This one serves to indulge, to entertain, to ingratiate. Anything goes when the whistle blows. Nothing is undone, nothing withheld—but it's all *hyper*, there is no continuity. Physical exchange is *escape from reality*.

GUIDELINES

You can get hurt. This combination is unstable. Play this one *short term*.

This combination is in Group D.
Turn to page 381.
Italicized words further
explained in the glossary.

Venus in Capricorn and Mars in Cancer

ROMANCE

starts slowly. Combining elements are working: receptive earth and pulsating water. This one is synchronized—with balance, control, direction. There is nothing frivolous, nothing rash. This one is mature, intelligent, intuitive. This one can see, can steer, can cope, can manage. This one is parental. There is sympathy, compassion. The style is conciliatory. There is grace. The beat is steady. There is a richness. Romance builds, has meaning. The heart is good. Cool magical waters flow from a deep underground spring.

LOVE

grows. Affections are constant, emotions are deep. This one relates to love, is motivated by love, holds on to love, protects love, reaches fulfillment through love. This one is devotional, enduring. There is honor, purpose . . . music, wine. This one is all things dear. Something is lush, with rare quality. The harvest moon is radiant.

PASSION

is *tremendous*. This one communicates by touch, serves
to replenish, to comfort, to nurture. There is a sublime
cresting. This one knows nerve centers, is *uncanny*.
Nothing is denied—it's all *ultra*. There is continuity.
Physical exchange is *culmination of love*.

GUIDELINES

You can't get hurt. This combination is stable (one love at
a time). Play this one *long term*.

This combination is in Group **A**.
Turn to page 375.
Italicized words further
explained in the glossary.

Venus in Capricorn
and
Mars in Leo

ROMANCE

is *erratic*. Opposite elements are working: dense earth and uncontrolled fire. There is inner turmoil—no restraint. Impulse propels, ego adds to the speed, boldness takes this one too far out. There are shocks, collisions, entanglements. There is no intuition, no discretion. Romance can't build, can't grow. This one is dynamite with an unpredictable fuse.

LOVE

is *chaotic*. Affections are extravagant, emotions are theatrical. This one is brash, overbearing, demanding, too aggressive—gives too much, requires too much. There is no patience, no finesse, no rhythm, no timing. There are flare-ups. This one is unknowing. There is no music, no substance . . . the beat is disjointed . . . love can't survive. It's all anti-climactic. There is nobody home.

PASSION

is *tumultuous*. Pent-up energies are released. This one serves to indulge, to entertain, to ingratiate. There is awesome surge. Nothing is undone, nothing is withheld—but it's all *hyper*, it's all confused. Physical exchange is *escape from reality*.

GUIDELINES

You can get hurt. This combination is unstable. Play this one *short term*.

This combination is in Group D.
Turn to page 381.
Italicized words further
explained in the glossary.

Venus in Capricorn and Mars in Virgo

ROMANCE

starts slowly. Similar elements are working. This one is receptive, soft earth. The style is easy—inner systems are finely tuned. There is nothing flamboyant, nothing frivolous. This one is quiet, efficient, controlled, balanced, reserved, methodical, practical, realistic. There is tact, discretion. This one knows how to accommodate, how to defer, when to yield. This one is supple, has rhythm. The beat is subtle. It's all with grace, intelligence. Romance sustains, romance builds. This skillful sheriff keeps the peace without guns.

LOVE

grows. Affections are low-keyed, emotions are constant. This one is equal to love, takes care of love, can manage love. This one is intuitive—can see, can anticipate, can steer. This one is unflappable, can handle pressure, can handle turbulence, can handle emergencies. This one keeps love together, gets the job done. It's all with understanding, all sophisticated, all honest. Life emerges. The earth is permissive—there is a greening, a blooming.

PASSION

is *tremendous*. This one communicates by touch, serves to comfort, to indulge, to assure. This one responds to need, knows nerve centers, is *uncanny*. Nothing is denied—it's all well-intentioned, all high-level. There is continuity. Physical exchange is *expression of faith*.

GUIDELINES

You can't get hurt. This combination is stable (one love at a time). Play this one *long term*.

This combination is in Group B.
Turn to page 377.
Italicized words further
explained in the glossary.

Venus in Capricorn and Mars in Libra

ROMANCE

is *erratic*. Opposite elements are working: dense earth and prodigal air. Inner systems are disorganized. This one is quickly persuaded, easily tempted, quickly fascinated. Impulse propels, lack of restraint adds to the speed, pursuit of excitement takes this one too far out. There is recklessness, scatter-shot judgment, no direction. The beat is wild—this one spins. There are entanglements, mad flights. Romance can't build, has no depth. This one is quick-passing disruptive whirl-wind.

LOVE

is *chaotic*. Affections are quick-erupting, emotions are uncontrolled. This one is driven... pursues love, lives to love... but doesn't know love, can't deal with reality, dreams fantastic dreams. This one is futile, tossed, theatrical, contrived. There is no stature. Love can't grow—this one can't manage love. This one is a sparrow in the costume of an eagle.

LOVE

is *tumultuous*. Pent-up energies are released. This one serves to indulge, to lavish, to ingratiate. This one knows touch, is *uncanny*. There is something bizarre. Nothing is undone, nothing withheld, but it's all confused, all *hyper*. Physical exchange is *pursuit of fantasy*.

GUIDELINES

You can get hurt. This combination is unstable. Play this one *short term*.

This combination is in Group C.
Turn to page 379.
Italicized words further
explained in the glossary.

Venus in Capricorn and Mars in Scorpio

ROMANCE

starts slowly. Combining elements are working: receptive earth and surging water. This one is magnetic—has power, sympathy, compassion, dedication. This one is supportive, adult, intelligent, ultra-intuitive, reliable, protective, fearless. This one can navigate. There is something mystical. This one hears a distant song, steers by a distant star. The beat is strong—romance builds, has profound meaning. Something is unstoppable.

LOVE

grows. Affections are warm, emotions are deep. This one is designed for love, propelled by love, fulfilled by love. There is nothing whimsical, nothing stupid. This one knows how to give, has poise, blends devotion with humor. There is confidence, sophistication, taste, charm, grace—rare ingenuity, rare perspective. This one is irresistible. Love is in marvelous hands. The wine is superb.

PASSION

is *tremendous*. This one communicates by touch, serves to replenish, to lavish, to nurture. The juices flow—there is a voluptuousness. This one knows nerve centers, is *uncanny*. Nothing is denied. It's all high-level; there is continuity. Physical exchange is *rendezvous with destiny*.

GUIDELINES

You can't get hurt. This combination is stable (one love at a time). Play this one *long term*.

This combination is in Group B.
Turn to page 377.
Italicized words further
explained in the glossary.

Venus in Capricorn and Mars in Sagittarius

ROMANCE

is *erratic*. Opposite elements are working: dense earth and unrestricted fire. This one is unpredictable, uncaring—flippant, shallow, hard to reach. There is abandon, recklessness, nothing abiding. This one gambles. Restlessness propels, indiscretion adds to the speed, lack of honesty takes this one too far out. This one is an alley cat. There are no convictions. This one is jaded—there is something perverse. Romance can't build—there is no direction, no aspiration. The flame flickers and dies quickly.

LOVE

is *chaotic*. Affections are theatrical, emotions are thin. This one doesn't relate to love, has no interest in love, doesn't know love, doesn't want to know love. This one lives outside the rules—the renegade, the artful dodger. There are opportunistic commitments, entanglements. This one is nimble, adventurous, superficial, deceitful. Love can't grow, can't survive. There is a mad flight to nowhere.

PASSION

is *tumultuous*. Pent-up energies are released. This one serves to indulge, to entertain, to ingratiate. Anything goes when the whistle blows. Nothing is undone, nothing withheld. It's all fleeting, all *hyper*; there is no continuity. Physical exchange is *escape from reality*.

GUIDELINES

You can get hurt. This combination is unstable. Play this one *short term*.

This combination is in Group D.
Turn to page 381.
Italicized words further
explained in the glossary.

Venus in Capricorn
and
Mars in Capricorn

ROMANCE

starts slowly. Exact same elements are working: all
receptive earth. This one is magnetic. There is
warmth, depth. This one operates intelligently, with
intuition, timing. This one knows the art of romance—
knows when to bend, when to defer, how to reduce
pressure, how to assure. This one uses power
strategically, with humor, with grace. The sap rises,
there are buddings.

LOVE

grows. Affections are smooth-flowing, emotions are
deep. This one lives to love, to manage love. This one is
rugged, devoted, parental—a practical entrepreneur.
This one can steer, can keep the thing interesting, can
keep it ongoing. There is a talent to amuse, a talent to
survive. Love is in good hands: there is texture,
purpose, character.

PASSION

is *tremendous*. This one communicates by touch, serves to indulge, to replenish, to nurture. The senses reel. This one knows nerve centers, is *uncanny*. Nothing is denied. It's all high-level, all well-intentioned. There is continuity. Physical exchange is *rendezvous with destiny*.

GUIDELINES

You can't get hurt. This combination is stable (one love at a time). Play this one *long term*.

This combination is in Group B.
Turn to page 377.
Italicized words further
explained in the glossary.

Venus in Capricorn
and
Mars in Aquarius

ROMANCE

is *erratic*. Opposite elements are working: dense earth
and uncontainable air. Inner systems are disorganized.
This one is pliable, gullible, impressionable . . . has no
intuition, no timing . . . can't see, can't steer, can't
cope. There are instant involvements, instant commitments. There is no control, no restraint, no
judgment—confusion. This one spins, hapless, tossed.
Romance can't build, can't grow. This one is a
rambling tumbleweed.

LOVE

is *chaotic*. Affections are superficial, emotions are thin.
This one is amateur. Idealism propels, impulse adds to
the speed, lack of discretion takes this one too far out.
There are catastrophes. This one is vulnerable,
bewildered, unfulfilled. This one can't manage. There
is something masochistic. Love can't grow, love can't
sustain. There is abandon—riding a toboggan blind-
folded.

PASSION

is *tumultuous*. Pent-up energies are released. This one serves to indulge, to lavish, to ingratiate. Anything goes when the whistle blows. This one knows nerve centers, is *uncanny*. Nothing is undone, nothing withheld—it's all *hyper*, there is no continuity. Physical exchange is *escape from reality*.

GUIDELINES

You can get hurt. This combination is unstable. Play this one *short term*.

This combination is in Group D.
Turn to page 381.
Italicized words further
explained in the glossary.

Venus in Capricorn and Mars in Pisces

ROMANCE

starts slowly. Combining elements are working: receptive earth and gentle water. This one is calm, soft, peaceful, honest, refined. There is control, balance, direction, timing. This one is reliable, sympathetic, intuitive. This one knows how to build. This one keeps the thing going smoothly, with intelligence, understanding. This one can cope, can steer. Romance emerges; it is in good hands. This one is a pond where small creatures come to drink sweet, cool water.

LOVE

grows. Affections are inspired, emotions are devotional. This one is supportive, contributing, nurturing. This one operates low-key, with diligence and perseverance. This one is the modest, capable entrepreneur—knows how to give, when to give...how to yield, when to yield...how to orchestrate. Love has depth, love endures. There is magical rhythm, the music swells, the call is clear. Something is irresistible.

PASSION

is *tremendous*. This one communicates by touch, serves to comfort, to replenish, to assure. This one responds to need. The juices flow. This one is *uncanny*. Nothing is denied. It's all high-level; there is continuity. Physical exchange is *expression of faith*.

GUIDELINES

You can't get hurt. This combination is stable (one love at a time). Play this one *long term*.

This combination is in Group B.
Turn to page 377.
Italicized words further
explained in the glossary.

Venus in Aquarius
and
Mars in Aries

ROMANCE

starts quickly. Combining elements are working: clear
air and brilliant fire. This one is big, noble, balanced—
has momentum and confidence. There is nothing weak,
nothing cheap. This one gives to get, puts it all up. This
one is intelligent, knows romance, rises to romance,
brings strength to romance. There is unstoppable
idealism, an irresistible beat. The heart is good.
Something sparkles. There is shining purpose.

LOVE

is *good times*. Affections are ardent, emotions are deep.
This one can handle love—thrives on love. This one has
timing, intuition . . . knows how to support, when to
support . . . has the grace to yield, the depth to endure,
the character to keep building. This one is the
courageous entrepreneur, keeping love together. This
one is reliable, assuring, mature. There is richness,
majesty, grandeur.

PASSION

is *sacred duty*. This one is mental—serves to support, to inspire, to nurture. This one responds to need. There is straightforward release of energy. Nothing is denied. It's all high-level, all well-intentioned. There is continuity. Physical exchange is *rendezvous with destiny*.

GUIDELINES

You can't get hurt. This combination is stable (one love at a time). Play this one *long term*.

This combination is in Group B.
Turn to page 377.
Italicized words further
explained in the glossary.

Venus in Aquarius and Mars in Taurus

ROMANCE

is *erratic*. Opposite elements are working: uncontainable air and dense earth. Inner systems are disorganized. There are extremes; there is no timing. This one can't steer. Something drags—there is fear of rejection, inability to receive signals, muddled reception, confusion, entanglements. Romance can't build. This one is tossed, is uncontrolled, goes in all directions. The beat is wild; there is uncertainty.

LOVE

is *chaotic*. Affections are superficial, emotions are opportunistic. This one is contrived, can't play the game, can't give, can't receive, can't cope. There is no intuition, no confidence, no humor, nothing towering. This one is amateur, requires too much, understands too little—can't see. Love can't grow, love can't build. There is pain, catastrophe. The glitter fades. It's all dry, all anti-climactic.

PASSION

is *tumultuous*. Deep pent-up energies are released. This one serves to indulge, to entertain, to ingratiate. This one knows nerve centers, relates to touch, is *uncanny*. Nothing is undone, nothing is withheld, but it's all *hyper*—there is no continuity. Physical exchange is *pursuit of fulfillment*.

GUIDELINES

You can get hurt. This combination is unstable. Play this one *short term*.

This combination is in Group C.
Turn to page 379.
Italicized words further
explained in the glossary.

Venus in Aquarius
and
Mars in Gemini

ROMANCE

starts quickly. Similar elements are working: controlled, sparkling air. The style is graceful—charm, humor, character. Idealism propels, imagination adds to the speed. There is nothing frivolous, nothing low. This one is fast-moving but discriminating... curious but cautious... fascinated by romance, rises to romance, can handle romance, knows how to build romance. This one is irresistible. There is unstoppable enthusiasm, shining purpose. Romance takes wing. There is magic in the air.

LOVE

is *good times.* Affections are contained, emotions are deep. Love settles this one. This one relates to love—is supportive, contributive, reliable. There are no theatrics, no pressure. This one has timing, tact, intuition—can handle love, can cope. This one does best as a buddy, a pal, an ace-in-the-hole. It's all smooth-flowing, easy-going. Love sustains; the beat is steady. This one keeps it together.

PASSION

is *sacred duty*. This one is mental—serves to comfort, to assure, to inspire. This one responds to need. Nothing is denied. There is straightforward release of energy. It's all well-intentioned—there is continuity. Physical exchange is *expression of faith*.

GUIDELINES

You can't get hurt. This combination is stable (one love at a time). Play this one *long term*.

This combination is in Group B.
Turn to page 377.
Italicized words further
explained in the glossary.

Venus in Aquarius and Mars in Cancer

ROMANCE

is *erratic*. Opposite elements are working: uncontainable air and dense water. Inner systems are disorganized—no balance, no timing or rhythm, no intuition. This one is scattered, amateur, insecure...easily flattered, easily moved, easily fooled...can't see, can't steer, can't manage. There are entanglements, involvements. This one plays at romance, flirts with romance, can't build romance—goes around in circles. There is something unlucky. It rains at the picnic.

LOVE

is *chaotic*. Affections are theatrical, emotions are superficial. There is nothing generous, nothing towering—no grace, no inspiration. This one has trouble giving. There is something clumsy, heavy, unsophisticated. Possessed with self-concern, this one gropes, is maudlin, limited. There is no talent to amuse. Love spins, can't grow. The beat is hesitant.

PASSION

is *tumultuous*. Deep pent-up energies are released. This one serves to indulge, to entertain, to nurture. There is an outpouring. This one relates to touch. Nothing is undone, nothing withheld—it's all *hyper*, all confused. Physical exchange is *pursuit of fulfillment*.

GUIDELINES

You can get hurt. This combination is unstable. Play this one *short term*.

This combination is in Group C.
Turn to page 379.
Italicized words further
explained in the glossary.

Venus in Aquarius and Mars in Leo

ROMANCE

starts quickly. Similar elements are working: vibrant air and royal fire. This one is big—has power and color. Adventure propels, courage adds to the speed, chivalry adds to the charm. This one is warm, outgoing, generous, sporting, with humor. Romance builds; it is in honest hands. The beat is unstoppable. There is something Viking in the style.

LOVE

is *good times.* Affections are full, emotions are deep. This one is intelligent, can cope, can manage. There is nothing cheap, nothing theatrical. This one is reliable, caring, parental—rises to love, feeds love, projects love. There is glory, conviction, unconquerable idealism. Love grows, love sustains. The forces of good are unstoppable.

PASSION

is *sacred duty*. This one is mental—serves to replenish, to inspire, to nurture. This one responds to need, is intuitive, permissive. Nothing is denied. It's all high-level—there is grace, continuity. Physical exchange is *rendezvous with destiny*.

GUIDELINES

You can't get hurt. This combination is stable (one love at a time). Play this one *long term*.

This combination is in Group B.
Turn to page 377.
Italicized words further
explained in the glossary.

Venus in Aquarius
and
Mars in Virgo

ROMANCE

is *erratic*. Opposite elements are working: uncontainable air and barren earth. Inner systems are disorganized, with no direction, no flair, no rhythm. This one is pliable, naive, gullible—too accessible, too permissive, too impulsive. There are instant commitments, misplaced loyalties, entanglements. The beat is uncertain. Romance spins, can't build. There is confusion, madness.

LOVE

is *chaotic*. Affections are scattered, emotions are sincere. Good-intentions propel, willingness to please adds to the speed, lack of judgment takes this one too far out. There is no control. This one can't anticipate, can't see, can't steer, can't manage. This one gives too much too soon. There is no timing. This one is too quickly dedicated, too quickly compliant, too selfless. There is no confidence. Love can't build, can't sustain. There is something melancholy. This one is unlucky— a fawn lost in the dark forest.

PASSION

is *tumultuous*. Pent-up energies are released. This one serves to indulge, to replenish, to ingratiate. Anything goes when the whistle blows. This one knows nerve centers. There is erotic intuition. Nothing is undone, nothing withheld—it's all *hyper*, there is no continuity. Physical exchange is *escape from reality*.

GUIDELINES

You can get hurt. This combination is unstable. Play this one *short term*.

This combination is in Group D.
Turn to page 381.
Italicized words further
explained in the glossary.

Venus in Aquarius and Mars in Libra

ROMANCE

starts quickly. Similar elements are working: soft perfumed air—intoxicating. There is refinement, finesse, sophistication, grace. Idealism propels, imagination adds to the speed, intelligence adds to the charm. This one has rhythm, confidence, humor. This one is designed for romance—brings sparkle, color and tempo to romance. There is a magical soaring. These winds are exotic. This one pursues a rare dream.

LOVE

is *good times.* Affections are controlled, emotions are deep. This one knows love, relates to love, builds love, rises to love. There is richness, purpose, maturity—nothing frivolous, nothing uncertain. This one keeps love together, steers through turbulence, can handle pressure—has the talent to cope, to anticipate, to orchestrate. This one is super-balanced, irresistible, sublime. Love reaches new heights. This one shapes destiny.

PASSION

is *tremendous.* This one is mental—serves to assure, to inspire, to nurture. This one is intuitive, knows nerve centers. There is a transcendence. Nothing is denied. It's all high-level; there is continuity. Physical exchange is *rendezvous with destiny.*

GUIDELINES

You can't get hurt. This combination is stable (one love at a time). Play this one *long term.*

This combination is in Group B.
Turn to page 377.
Italicized words further
explained in the glossary.

Venus in Aquarius and Mars in Scorpio

ROMANCE

is *erratic*. Opposite elements are working: uncontainable air and uncontrolled water. Inner systems are disorganized. This one is driven by obsessions, extremes. There is no rhythm, no direction, no restraint. There is something vagabond. This one plays a wild game, maneuvers. Romance is just a tool. Something irresistible calls. The beat is wild, the music is frenzied. This one can't stop dancing.

LOVE

is *chaotic*. Affections are whimsical, emotions are limited. There is no kindred spirit, no warmth, nothing towering, no discretion. There are involvements, entanglements. This one is disruptive—doesn't care, has no aspirations. This one doesn't relate to love, uses love. Something is corrupt. This is one manipulated by powers of darkness.

PASSION

is *tumultuous*. Deep pent-up energies are released. This one serves to indulge, to lavish, to ingratiate. Anything goes when the whistle blows. The juices flow. This one is *uncanny*. Nothing is undone, nothing withheld. This one is bizarre. It's all *hyper*, all confused, without continuity. Physical exchange is *escape from reality*.

GUIDELINES

You can get hurt. This combination is unstable. Play this one *short term*.

This combination is in Group D.
Turn to page 381.
Italicized words further
explained in the glossary.

Venus in Aquarius
and
Mars in Sagittarius

ROMANCE

starts quickly. Combining elements are working: vibrant air and low-keyed fire. The style is easy, friendly. This one has humor, rhythm, suppleness. There is nothing flamboyant, nothing theatrical. This one has character, gives more than is received. There are good intentions. The winds are gentle, the fires are cool. The beat is steady, there is a blending...romance grows and builds...the spirit rises. There is shining promise.

LOVE

is *good times*. Affections are controlled, emotions are mature. This one is intelligent, can manage—knows love, protects love, is inspired by love, is equal to love. This one has the knack, discretion, tact. This one is sympathetic, forgiving, loyal, liberal, intuitive—knows how to support, when to support. There is nothing superficial. The heart is good. This one knows how to survive. Love endures. This one is a trooper, a soldier, a keeper of the keys.

PASSION

is *sacred duty*. This one is mental—serves to assure, to comfort, to inspire. This one responds to need. There is a permissiveness. This one is therapeutic. Nothing is denied. It's all high-level, all well-intentioned; there is continuity. Physical exchange is *expression of faith*.

GUIDELINES

You can't get hurt. This combination is stable (one love at a time). Play this one *long term*.

This combination is in Group B.
Turn to page 377.
Italicized words further
explained in the glossary.

Venus in Aquarius
and
Mars in Capricorn

ROMANCE

is *erratic*. Opposite elements are working: uncontainable air and dense earth. Inner systems are disorganized, with no balance, no rhythm, nothing aspirational. This one gropes, can't steer. Impulse propels, lack of restraint adds to the speed, lack of intuition takes this one too far out. There are catastrophes, entanglements. It's all a blind search, a waste of energy. Romance doesn't sustain, can't build. Something haunts, something is anti-climactic. The party is over but this one can't stop dancing.

LOVE

is *chaotic*. Affections are scattered, emotions are primitive. This one doesn't relate to love. There is no depth, nothing warm, nothing abiding. This one is tossed, driven, obsessed—dry, gross. There is nothing auspicious. The beat is disjointed, the music is discordant. Love has no chance. There are only shadows; nobody's home.

PASSION

is *tumultuous*. Pent-up energies are released. This one serves to indulge, to lavish, to ingratiate. Anything goes when the whistle blows. This one knows nerve centers, has erotic intuition, is *uncanny*. It's all confused, all *hyper*—there is no continuity. Physical exchange is *escape from reality*.

GUIDELINES

You can get hurt. This combination is unstable. Play this one *short term*.

This combination is in Group D.
Turn to page 381.
Italicized words further
explained in the glossary.

Venus in Aquarius
and
Mars in Aquarius

ROMANCE

starts quickly. Exact same elements are working. This one is all vibrant air. The style is easy, sporting, sociable, liberal. There is nothing cheap, nothing superficial. This one has character, humor, imagination. Pursuit of adventure propels, courage adds to the speed, intelligence adds to the charm. This one has rhythm and direction—relates to romance, brings brilliance to romance. There is beauty of purpose. It's all rewarding. The beat is firm. There is confidence, chivalry. Something shines, something is irrepressible. There is cheerful comradery.

LOVE

is *good times.* Affections are evenly released, emotions are deep. There is a wholesome attitude, something rugged. This one is reliable, mature—can steer, can cope. There is intuition, sympathy, compassion. This one relates to family, takes care of love, rises to love ... is strong, has conviction ... is unswerving, unbending, undaunted. This one is train tracks beyond the horizon.

346

PASSION

is *sacred duty*. This one is mental—serves to comfort, to assure, to inspire. This one responds to need, knows nerve centers. Nothing is denied. It's all well-intentioned, all high-level—there is continuity. Physical exchange is *expression of faith*.

GUIDELINES

You can't get hurt. This combination is stable (one love at a time). Play this one *long term*.

This combination is in Group B.
Turn to page 377.
Italicized words further
explained in the glossary.

Venus in Aquarius and Mars in Pisces

ROMANCE

is *erratic*. Opposite elements are working: uncontainable air and uncontrolled water. Inner systems are disorganized—no balance, no direction, no restraint. This one is too accessible, too quickly permissive, too quickly yielding, amateur, hapless, indiscriminate. There is wild idealism, no intuition, no depth. This one can't steer. Romance can't build; it is just a word. This one is deceptive. There is bad seed. Aspirations are bankrupt. This one is tossed, lost, jaded. There is madness. This one spins headlong into catastrophes.

LOVE

is *chaotic*. Affections are shallow, emotions are theatrical. This one is opportunistic, self-serving, corrupt—plays at love, draws from love, uses love. There is nothing uplifting, nothing fulfilling. It's all a futile odyssey, total abandon. There are entanglements, confusion. There is no ore. This one is buffeted, parasitic: a leech clings, a tick digs in. This one can't give. There is no vision, no expanse, no capacity to shape destiny. The beat is wild. This one rides the doomsday rocket.

PASSION

is *tumultuous*. Pent-up energies are released. This one serves to indulge, to entertain, to ingratiate. Anything goes when the whistle blows. Nothing is undone, nothing is withheld. It's all *hyper*, without meaning or continuity. Physical exchange is *escape from reality*.

GUIDELINES

You can get hurt. This combination is unstable. Play this one *short term*.

This combination is in Group D.
Turn to page 381.
Italicized words further
explained in the glossary.

Venus in Pisces
and
Mars in Aries

ROMANCE

is *erratic*. Opposite elements are working: churning water and scorching fire. Inner systems are disorganized. This one can't resist challenge . . . is impatient, forceful, demanding . . . gives too much too soon, requires too much too soon. Pursuit of adventure takes this one up, ego adds to the speed, recklessness takes this one down. This one is imprudent, has no rhythm, no timing, no intuition. Romance can't build. There are shocks, entanglements, catastrophes. This one stays on board the burning ship too long.

LOVE

is *chaotic*. Affections are eruptive, emotions are stormy. This one is too ardent, too fierce, too domineering to handle love. There is possessiveness, jealousy. There are tempests. This one is exhausting, exacting, too intense—without humor, without sympathy, without understanding or grace. Love can't survive. Small fish float belly-up after underwater explosions.

PASSION

is *tumultuous*. Pent-up energies are released. This one serves to conquer, to entertain, to nurture. There is awesome surge. Nothing is undone, nothing withheld—it's all *hyper*, all confused. Physical exchange is *pursuit of fantasy*.

GUIDELINES

You can get hurt. This combination is unstable. Play this one *short term*.

This combination is in Group C.
Turn to page 379.
Italicized words further
explained in the glossary.

Venus in Pisces and Mars in Taurus

ROMANCE

starts slowly. Combining elements are working: sweet water and pulsating earth. This one is honorable, gentle, enduring . . . balanced, controlled, directed . . . sympathetic, diplomatic, reliable. This one has tact and discretion—knows how to support, how to build. This one has timing, patience, determination, can cope, can manage. Romance is in steady hands. There is substance, grace, humor, color, beauty of purpose, richness. Romance builds. The wine flows.

LOVE

grows. Affections are rich, emotions are deep. This one relates to love—is propelled by love, dedicated to love, equal to love. There is nothing weak, nothing frivolous. This one works efficiently, can orchestrate. This one is intelligent, with conviction. There is parental drive. This one keeps it together. The beat is unstoppable: this one shapes destiny. Small furry animals feed in safety. The sap rises, there is a vitality—the music of life.

PASSION

is *tremendous*. This one communicates by touch, serves to soothe, to replenish, to nurture. This one is intuitive, *uncanny*, knows nerve centers. Nothing is denied. It's all high-level; there is continuity. Physical exchange is *rendezvous with destiny*.

GUIDELINES

You can't get hurt. This combination is stable (one love at a time). Play this one *long term*.

This combination is in Group B.
Turn to page 377.
Italicized words further
explained in the glossary.

Venus in Pisces
and
Mars in Gemini

ROMANCE

is *erratic*. Opposite elements are working: uncontrolled water and restless air. This one is superficial, changeable, scattered. There is no balance, no finesse, no rhythm, no restraint—this one is quickly infatuated, easily tempted. Excitement propels, impulse adds to the speed, lack of direction takes this one too far out. There are shocks, entanglements, turmoil. This one spins. Romance can't build. This one is the ill wind that blows no good.

LOVE

is *chaotic*. Affections are thin, emotions are fleeting. This one is fickle, insincere, unfeeling, doesn't relate to love, hasn't the patience for love. There is no warmth, no sympathy, no kindred spirit. There are shallow commitments, maneuvers, games—it's all without meaning, without aspiration. This one is remote. There is something jaded. This one deals in illusion.

PASSION

is *tumultuous*. Pent-up energies are released. This one
serves to indulge, to entertain, to ingratiate. Anything
goes when the whistle blows. Nothing is undone,
nothing withheld. There are acrobatics. It's all
madness, all confused, all *hyper*; there is no continuity.
Physical exchange is *escape from reality*.

GUIDELINES

You can get hurt. This combination is unstable. Play this
one *short term*.

This combination is in Group D.
Turn to page 381.
Italicized words further
explained in the glossary.

Venus in Pisces
and
Mars in Cancer

ROMANCE

starts slowly. Similar elements are working. This one is all sweet, receptive water. Violins sing. This one is controlled, balanced, soft, kind, gentle, sociable. There is grace, depth. This one knows romance, knows how to shape romance. There is timing, taste, quality. This one requires time. Romance builds, distills. There is richness, beauty. Something pulses with promise. Fish in the sea dance a mystical ballet.

LOVE

grows. Affections are free-flowing, emotions are deep. This one is ultra-sympathetic, ultra-compassionate, ultra-intuitive. This one can cope, can anticipate, can manage. This one is parental—is propelled by love, requires love, is equal to love, swells to love, is fulfilled by love. These tides are irresistible. There is purpose, constancy. This one is organized, keeps love together. It's all with style, direction. There is something magical.

PASSION

is *tremendous*. This one communicates by touch, serves to replenish, to comfort, to nurture. This one is intuitive, knows nerve centers. Nothing is denied—it's all high-level, all well-intentioned. There is continuity. Physical exchange is *rendezvous with destiny*.

GUIDELINES

You can't get hurt. This combination is stable (one love at a time). Play this one *long term*.

This combination is in Group B.
Turn to page 377.
Italicized words further
explained in the glossary.

Venus in Pisces and Mars in Leo

ROMANCE

is *erratic*. Opposite elements are working: churning water and uncontrolled fire. Inner systems are disorganized—extreme, bombastic, overbearing. There is no balance, no discretion, no restraint. The beat is wild. Pursuit of adventure propels, impulse adds to the speed, over-confidence takes this one too far out. There is recklessness, madness, blustering. There are shocks, entanglements, possible violence. Romance can't build. A lion is loose in the streets.

LOVE

is *chaotic*. Affections are extravagant, emotions are theatrical. This one doesn't know love, has no feel for love. This one is big, empty, brash, domineering, vain, self-serving. There is no grace, no humor, no intuition, no imagination. This one is limited—can't steer, can't orchestrate, can't walk a straight line. This one is the sudden, erupting volcano.

PASSION

is *tumultuous*. Pent-up energies are released. This one
serves to indulge, to entertain, to ingratiate. Anything
goes when the whistle blows. Nothing is undone,
nothing withheld. It's all without meaning or
continuity, all *hyper*. Physical exchange is *escape from
reality*.

GUIDELINES

You can get hurt. This combination is unstable. Play this
one *short term*.

This combination is in Group D.
Turn to page 381.
Italicized words further
explained in the glossary.

Venus in Pisces
and
Mars in Virgo

ROMANCE
starts slowly. Combining elements are working: sweet water and receptive earth. There is peace, order, method. This one is soft, kind, gentle, yielding, well-intentioned, caring...patient, dedicated, enduring, selfless...intelligent, realistic. This one operates quietly—there is timing, ingenuity, rhythm. Romance builds, romance has quality. Something pulses with promise.

LOVE
grows. Affections are smooth-flowing, emotions are deep. This one relates to love, is equal to love—is persevering, reliable, consistent. There is nothing flamboyant, nothing frivolous. This one keeps the thing together, is organized. There is ease of manner, control, direction. This one can handle pressure, can cope, can manage. This one has purpose, has the knack—love is in good hands. The beat is steady. There is unflagging loyalty. There is the style of the long-distance runner.

PASSION

is *tremendous*. This one communicates by touch, serves to replenish, to comfort, to assure. This one is intuitive, *uncanny*, knows nerve centers. Nothing is denied. It's all high-level. There is continuity. Physical exchange is *expression of faith*.

GUIDELINES

You can't get hurt. This combination is stable (one love at a time). Play this one *long term*.

This combination is in Group B.
Turn to page 377.
Italicized words further
explained in the glossary.

Venus in Pisces and Mars in Libra

ROMANCE

is *erratic*. Opposite elements are working: uncontrolled water and prodigal air. Inner systems are disorganized. This one is wildly quixotic, with no balance, no restraint, no direction. Idealism propels, lack of discretion adds to the speed, lack of judgment takes this one too far out. This one believes too quickly, gives too quickly, yields too quickly. There are instant crusades, instant commitments. Lack of intuition is ruinous. There are shocks, entanglements. Romance can't build. This one spins, charging at windmills.

LOVE

is *chaotic*. Affections are whimsical, emotions are extreme. This one is in love with love—a dreamer. This one can't see, can't steer, can't manage. There is no rhythm, no timing, no sense of proportion. There is pain, disillusion. This one is lost. Love can't sustain, can't grow. There is wasted tenderness, wasted inventory, futility. The grapes die on the vine.

PASSION

is *tumultuous*. Deep pent-up energies are released. This one serves to indulge, to inspire, to nurture. This one is intuitive, knows nerve centers. Nothing is undone, nothing withheld—but it's all *hyper*, all confused. Physical exchange is *pursuit of fulfillment*.

GUIDELINES

You can get hurt. This combination is unstable. Play this one *short term*.

This combination is in Group C.
Turn to page 379.
Italicized words further
explained in the glossary.

Venus in Pisces
and
Mars in Scorpio

ROMANCE

starts slowly. Similar elements are working. This one is clear, surging water—magnetic, powerful, intelligent. This one knows how to build romance. There is balance, control. This one is intuitive, discreet, compassionate ... knows human nature ... knows how to give, to support, to cope, to manage. There is timing, rhythm, direction. Romance is magical. The oceans teem with life, the tides rise in blushing excitement, the waves dance to mystical music.

LOVE

grows. Affections are mature, emotions are deep. This one is more than equal to love, a shaper of events ... patient, subtle, competent ... fearless, irresistible, enduring. Love is in strong hands. This one keeps love safe, has the knack. There is substance, depth, sophistication. This one drives toward fulfillment. The beat is unstoppable.

PASSION

is *tremendous*. This one communicates by touch, serves to gratify, to comfort, to nurture. The juices flow. This one sends shivers, knows nerve centers, is *uncanny*. Nothing is denied—it's all high-level, all well-intentioned. There is continuity. Physical exchange is *rendezvous with destiny*.

GUIDELINES

You can't get hurt. This combination is stable (one love at a time). Play this one *long term*.

This combination is in Group B.
Turn to page 377.
Italicized words further
explained in the glossary.

Venus in Pisces
and
Mars in Sagittarius

ROMANCE

is *erratic*. Opposite elements are working: uncontrolled water and uncontrolled fire. This one is without discipline, restraint or direction. This one is impatient, compulsive, reckless, unpredictable. Impulse propels, lack of intuition adds to the speed, pursuit of excitement takes this one too far out. There are extremes, there is madness. The beat is wild. This one is promiscuous. Romance spins. There is no substance, nothing lyrical. This one settles for trifles.

LOVE

is *chaotic*. Affections are fleeting, emotions are superficial. This one is adventurous, fast-moving, footloose—requires freedom. There is helter-skelter movement, shallow involvement, entanglement, turmoil. Something is corrupt. Love can't build, can't grow. This one leaves behind a trail of wreckage.

PASSION

is *tumultuous*. Pent-up energies are released. This one serves to indulge, to entertain, to ingratiate. Anything goes when the whistle blows. Nothing is undone, nothing withheld. It's all without meaning or continuity, all *hyper*. Physical exchange is *escape from reality*.

GUIDELINES

You can get hurt. This combination is unstable. Play this one *short term*.

This combination is in Group D.
Turn to page 381.
Italicized words further
explained in the glossary.

Venus in Pisces and Mars in Capricorn

ROMANCE
starts slowly. Combining elements are working: clear water and receptive earth. There is strength, warmth, balance. This one knows romance, knows how to build romance. This one is intelligent—has discretion, poise, humor. Determination propels, convictions add to the speed. This one shapes destiny. The beat is confident. There is method, understanding, grace, rhythm, good intent. Romance pulsates. There is a fragrance, tempo, music, wine.

LOVE
grows. Affections are dutiful, emotions are deep. This one is designed for love, motivated by love. This one is organized, perceptive, intuitive. This one can cope, can manage, can orchestrate . . . has the knack . . . knows how to build, how to support. This one is protective, parental, courageous—has dignity, purpose, fulfillment. Love conquers all. Tropical islands rise from the sea.

PASSION
is *tremendous*. This one communicates by touch, serves
to replenish, to comfort, to nurture. The juices flow.
This one knows nerve centers, is *uncanny*. Nothing is
denied. It's all high-level; there is continuity. Physical
exchange is *rendezvous with destiny*.

GUIDELINES
You can't get hurt. This combination is stable (one love at
a time). Play this one *long term*.

This combination is in Group B.
Turn to page 377.
Italicized words further
explained in the glossary.

Venus in Pisces
and
Mars in Aquarius

ROMANCE

is *erratic*. Opposite elements are working: uncontrolled water and uncontainable air. Inner systems are disorganized. This one is vulnerable, gullible, unsophisticated. There is no direction, no intuition. This one can't see, can't cope, can't manage—is easily tempted, easily fooled. This one is tossed. There are shocks, disappointments, entanglements. This one is amateur. Romance doesn't sustain. This one is a young bird too far from the nest.

LOVE

is *chaotic*. Affections are impulsive, emotions are muddled. Enthusiasm propels, super-optimism takes this one up, lack of judgment takes this one down. There is no timing, no tact, no discretion. The style is too open, the spirit is too willing. This one is naive—doesn't know the game. There are instant crusades, instant commitments, but no strategy, no grand design. Love can't grow, love is lost. This one plays at life. Something haunts, something is anti-climactic.

PASSION

is *tumultuous*. Pent-up energies are released. This one serves to indulge, to entertain, to ingratiate. Anything goes when the whistle blows. This one is carnal, knows nerve centers. Nothing is undone, nothing withheld, but it's all *hyper*, all confused, without continuity— there is madness. Physical exchange is *escape from reality*.

GUIDELINES

You can get hurt. This combination is unstable. Play this one *short term*.

This combination is in Group D.
Turn to page 381.
Italicized words further
explained in the glossary.

Venus in Pisces
and
Mars in Pisces

ROMANCE

starts slowly. Exact same elements are working. This one is all sweet water, dedicated, mature. This one has depth, refinement, gentility. This one is sympathetic, receptive, intuitive, reliable. There is balance and direction. This one operates quietly, efficiently—with tact and discretion. The beat is steady, the style is easy. This one relates to romance, knows how to build romance. This one is a mystical refreshing mist. Something pulsates.

LOVE

grows. Affections are rich, emotions are deep. This one lives to love, loves to love, knows how to love . . . has the knack, finesse, timing . . . knows how to support, when to support, how to reduce pressure. This one can cope, can steer, can manage. This one is parental, devoted. The elements dance. The tides rise, the oceans swell to the pull of the moon.

PASSION

is *tremendous*. This one communicates by touch, serves to replenish, to comfort, to nurture. The juices flow. This one knows nerve centers, is *uncanny*. Nothing is denied—it's all high-level, all well-intentioned. There is continuity. Physical exchange is *rendezvous with destiny*.

GUIDELINES

You can't get hurt. This combination is stable (one love at a time). Play this one *long term*.

This combination is in Group B.
Turn to page 377.
Italicized words further
explained in the glossary.

GROUP A

This group brings something extra to stable combinations.

This group can sustain with unstable combinations.

These combinations are superbly designed to manage relationships.

This group is *ultra*.

The elements dance.

Venus and Mars are perfectly synchronized.

GROUP A CAN BLEND WITH ALL COMBINATIONS.

Did you use the correct birth date? See the glossary.

GROUP B

This group adds character and strength to stable combinations.

This group can sustain with most unstable combinations.

These combinations have the "stuff of life."

The elements are powerfully orchestrated.

Venus and Mars work together efficiently.

GROUP B CAN BLEND WITH GROUPS A, B AND C.

THERE IS THE POSSIBILITY GROUP B CAN BLEND WITH SOME COMBINATIONS IN GROUP D.

Did you use the correct birth date? See the glossary.

GROUP C

This group can sustain with stable combinations.

This group cannot sustain with unstable combinations.

These combinations are designed to supplement.

These combinations cannot manage relationships.

These combinations require the even rhythm of stable combinations.

This group is *hyper*.

The elements are tossed.

Venus and Mars do not work together smoothly.

GROUP C CAN BLEND WITH GROUPS A AND B.

GROUP C DOES NOT BLEND WITH GROUPS C AND D.

Did you use the correct birth date? See the glossary.

GROUP D

This group can sustain with a few stable combinations.

This group cannot sustain with most combinations.

These combinations are not designed for relationships.

These combinations have no capacity for continuity.

This group is very *hyper*.

The elements are scattered.

Venus and Mars are totally opposed.

GROUP D CAN BLEND WITH COMBINATIONS IN GROUP A.

GROUP D MAY BLEND WITH SOME COMBINATIONS IN GROUP B.

GROUP D DOES NOT BLEND WITH GROUPS C OR D.

THERE IS THE POSSIBILITY THAT A COMBINATION IN THIS GROUP CANNOT BLEND WITH ANY COMBINATION.

Did you use the correct birth date? See the glossary.

E. Karlin

The Glossary

The glossary gives more information about each combination. It explains key words and phrases italicized throughout the combinations, and offers explanations of whatever you may not understand in the guide. The glossary explains things you may not understand about astrology. It completes the picture. Check the glossary for each new combination.

Aquarius	is a low-intensity male air sign.
Aries	is a high-intensity male fire sign.
astrology	is the study of the aspects of planets as they were placed in the signs at time of birth and how it relates to the variations of characteristics in human nature.
Cancer	is a high-intensity female water sign.
Capricorn	is a medium-intensity female earth sign.
chaotic	indicates an inability to live with love; a constant state of turbulence.
combination	is a Venus and Mars aspect.

complicated	indicates the push-pull effect of powerful positive elements that are conflicting; good intentions may be camouflaged; romance may be hard to understand, hard to handle.
culmination of love	is all elements in perfect harmony; brilliance of energy and purpose.
does better	indicates the probability of high-quality opposite elements working to sustain, to build, to make the thing good.
erratic	indicates inability to begin a relationship rhythmically; a lack of gamesmanship.
escape from reality	is a flight to nowhere; unregulated release of energy; passion without purpose; abandon.
expression of faith	is the payment of dues; a willingness to please; the capacity to give or receive whatever is required.
Gemini	is a medium-intensity male air sign.

good times	indicates that Venus and Mars are both in male signs—love has tempo, speed, vitality; energy is released enthusiastically.
grows	indicates that Venus and Mars are both in female signs—love is subtle, soft, restrained; energy is modulated.
hyper	is high highs and low lows.
Leo	is a medium-intensity male fire sign.
Libra	is a high-intensity male air sign.
long term	advises to stay; play for the long haul; keep the faith; hang on to something good.
Mars	is a male planet that describes desire and force of energy.
Pisces	is a low-intensity female water sign.
pursuit of fantasy	is a mad fling at fulfillment resulting in disillusion; an inability to see clearly; a rush to a mirage.

pursuit of fulfillment	is a release of idealistic energy; the motivation to deliver or receive honorably.
rendezvous with destiny	is all elements falling into place; a fulfilling release of energy.
sacred duty	is the call to deliver relief whenever required.
Sagittarius	is a low-intensity male fire sign.
Scorpio	is a medium-intensity female water sign.
short term	advises to be on guard; be ready to run; just a party—nothing that lasts—a weekend—an every-other-Thursday fling.
signs	are the twelve magnetic fields through which the planets travel, each planet operates differently as it passes through each magnetic field.
starts quickly	indicates that Venus and Mars are both in male signs—the style is spirited,

open, fast-moving; love at
first sight is a possibility.

starts slowly indicates that Venus and
Mars are both in female
signs—the style is recep-
tive, soft, sub-surface;
romance unfolds quietly,
the tempo is measured.

sun signs describe people outwardly.

Taurus is a high-intensity female
earth sign.

The Charts (pp. 1-73) locate what signs Venus
and Mars were in every day
for 70 years, from 1895 to
1965.

tremendous indicates an even release of
sexual energy, the capacity
to deliver or receive fully,
a rhythm, a divine pa-
tience.

tumultuous indicates uneven release of
sexual energy.

ultra is a steady high-planed
state of being; a divine
orchestration of spirit and
will.

uncanny	indicates the mysterious, mystical capacity to deliver powerful erotic sensations.
Venus	is a female planet that describes affections.
Virgo	is a low-intensity female earth sign.
you can get hurt	indicates commitment to an unstable combination can result in frustration, disappointment, pain.
you can't get hurt	indicates commitment to a stable combination is a good gamble; there is nothing unpredictable, nothing deceptive; minimal emotional danger.

Overview

Each planet has a special force.

Each sign has a special nature.

To cast a horoscope is to find in what signs the planets were placed at birth and to analyze the relationships of the planets as they are placed in the signs.

The relationships are aspects.

(If the Sun and Moon aspect is harmonious the outer image is smooth—assured—confident—winning.

If the Mercury and Uranus aspect is harmonious the intelligence is balanced—organized—logical—superior.

An unaspected Sun and Moon and a well-aspected Mercury and Uranus would result in an erratic outer image yet there would be inner mental balance.)

It's all in the aspects.

You cannot see aspects.

That is why people are hardly ever as they seem to be.

There are major and minor aspects.

The Venus and Mars aspect is major.

The Venus and Mars aspect prevails with respect to romance, love and passion, no matter the influence of any other aspect.

Keep the Guide with you.

The Guide could be your best friend.

Astrology is marvelous.

The Best of
Berkley's Nonfiction